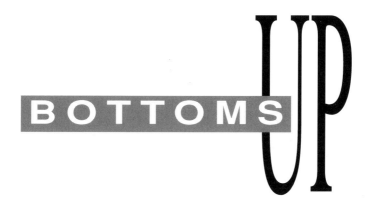

# BOTTOMS UP

*The complete voyages of the Lady Jane*

## ROBERT WATSON

*fernhurst*
**BOOKS**

First published in Great Britain as a series of stories entitled 'The Voyages of the Good Ship Lady Jane' and 'Lady Jane Sails Again' in *Motor Boat and Yachting* between December 1991 and June 1993 (except chapters 2 & 16).

First published in book form in 1994 by Fernhurst Books, Duke's Path, High Street, Arundel, West Sussex BN18 9AJ.

ISBN 1 898660 03 4

A British Library Cataloguing in Publication record for this book is available from the British Library.

**Acknowledgements**
Cartoons by Ian Dicks and Martin Fish.
Cover design by Simon Balley
DTP by Percy Halfwit

Printed and bound in Great Britain by Ebenezer Baylis & Son

# CONTENTS

# 1

# DRUMSALLAGH TO KILLYBAY

For those of you with a map, it should not be too hard to figure out that this is not much of a voyage, Drumsallagh being twenty miles from the sea and not on much of a river to speak of. Nevertheless, a voyage of some adventure it became.

The skipper, SJ, never a man to do things by halves, had ordered a low-loader to transport the Lady Jane to the sea. Forty-five feet of gleaming white paintwork, she perched incongruously on the lorry, waiting for the journey to her destiny. Alf, the driver, was a little bit worried.

"Shouldn't we take off that mast thing?" he asked timidly. Most people were timid round SJ.

"*****!" was the considered reply, and the mast thing stayed on.

Most of the telephones in County Carrick did not stay on that day, however. Lady Jane serenely took out every low wire that had the audacity to get in her way. This was a sign of things to come as we hurriedly covered our tracks and left the damage for someone else to clear up. Safely on the quayside, apart from a little scraped paintwork, we waited for the crane to sling the refitted boat into the water.

"What weight is she?" the crane-driver asked cautiously as he eyed the solid steel hull.

What weight can you lift?" SJ just as cautiously replied.

"About fifteen ton. That's what she's plated to, anyway."

"Aw, you're safe enough here then. She's well under that."

Maybe she was - before the refit, and before the loading

of three hundred gallons of fuel (cheaper for agricultural than marine, SJ had said), five hundred gallons of water, and six bottles of rum. All seemed well as the hull lifted off the lorry. It stayed well until she was about six feet above the water, when the crane started to show a definite list.

"I can't hold her!" the crane driver shouted.

"Well let her bloody go then!" SJ shouted back.

When the spray cleared, she was floating beautifully. The blue line dividing the white superstructure from the red anti-foul was exactly on the water for its entire length. She looked every inch a lady.

"Do you want to come on the maiden voyage?" SJ asked me.

Circumstances were against me. I had to get home for my tea; my wife was waiting; we were supposed to be

going out that night; it was just not possible. In the circumstances I gave the only answer that a sensible, sane man could give. "Yes, please," I said.

All went well as we cleared the quay and headed round the town rock. The twin Perkins engines were barking healthily, water was coming from both exhausts, and all systems were go. Down the lough we sailed - SJ, Knot, Eagle Eye and myself - for a couple of miles, then we described a large circle and headed back to port. Who would have launched a boat without first arranging a mooring? SJ would. What's more he had.

The first of many new enemies was made as he selected a mooring at random and instructed the crew to make fast to it. We had hardly settled back to enjoy our liquid refreshments when there was a bang on the hull, followed by an irate voice calling: "Anyone on board?"

"See what he wants," SJ instructed, so I stuck my head out of the wheelhouse door.

"Hello," I said, rather inadequately.

A small, dapper man was looking up at me from where he stood in his row-boat. His knuckles showed white against the mahogany rail but his face was the colour of beetroot.

"Hello?" he squeaked indignantly. "What do you mean by it, sir?"

I waited, hoping for some further information, then asked: "What seems to be the problem?"

"Problem? I'll give you problem. What do you mean by tying up to my mooring?"

Realisation dawned. I had just clicked into gear with a fairly good collection of lies when SJ decided to take a hand.

"What does the ***** want?" he growled, sticking his head out past me and glaring at Beetroot-face.

"I'll tell you what I want," our new little friend snapped back. "I want you off my mooring. And I want you off now."

SJ stepped out of the wheelhouse and over to the rail. The little man sat down hurriedly and rowed off into the gathering gloom, hurling abuse as he went.

A council of war was held at the saloon table. "We'll have to move," I said.

"For him?" SJ said, "Not bloody likely!"

Knot - who was well versed in SJ's thought processes - came up with the argument which changed his mind.

"That wee man could come back during the night and cut us loose."

"I knew to look at him that he couldn't be trusted." SJ declared. "I have a good mind to take his mooring with us. That would teach him not to go round cutting people adrift."

SJ, Knot and Eagle Eye finished another bottle of rum before we decided to find a new mooring. The evening air was decidedly chilly as we poured on deck to scout the available territory. After the bright lights of the saloon it took us a few minutes to adjust to the now almost pitch darkness. Eagle Eye was put on the searchlight, while the rest of us gazed hopefully for a vacant buoy.

"We need a visitor's mooring." Knot suggested.

"What are they like, then?" SJ asked.

"They're yellow, with 'visitor' written on them" Knot explained patiently.

"Nobody likes a smart ****." SJ said, his voice fading as he wandered back to the stern to have a pee,

"There's one!" Eagle Eye shouted, living up to his name.

As the only man completely sober, I was selected to stand at the bow, direct the helmsman and hook the mooring when we got close enough. This, of course, meant that a drunk was in total control of 300-odd horse-power. Well, three drunks really. Eagle Eye was at the rail - just outside the wheelhouse - relaying my directions. Knot was at the wheel, while SJ worked the throttles and countermanded my commands.

"He's blind," I could hear SJ mutter every few minutes. "The stupid git's blind."

Despite the confusion, I eventually managed to hook a mooring buoy - with 'visitor' written on it - and called for the engines to be stopped. SJ decided to help by putting them full astern instead. Luckily I was able to let go before having my arm ripped off.

"Hold on to the bloody thing next time!" SJ yelled. This time there was too much way on, and I went galloping down the deck holding on for grim death, almost knocking Eagle Eye overboard on the way past - then back again, as once more the engines went full astern.

Safely tied up, another bottle was broached and we sat in a companionable silence, each thinking his own thoughts.

"Well, it didn't go too bad," SJ said eventually. A strange observation in the circumstances but, unfortunately, prophetic.

# 2

## FISHING

There were four of us on board that fine summer after-noon: SJ, Joe, Steve and myself. Joe was a retired civil servant who had been out in the Lady Jane before but, as he said afterwards, "It was so long ago that I forgot to be sensible and say no."

This was Steve's first trip and he innocently thought it was going to be a pleasure one. No pirate captain or Captain Bligh could have been so insensitive to his crews' feelings as was SJ As soon as we were on board we were his, to order and to do his will. SJ expected total obedience from the crew, and woe betide anyone who did not jump when he spoke.

Things went fairly smoothly for the first half hour or so. We had launched the dinghy at Killybay harbour and Steve and I had gone out to bring the Lady Jane in to the wall. So far as possible SJ never travelled in the dinghy. Tide permitting he would be picked up at the beginning of a trip and dropped off at the end . The Lady Jane was never allowed to sail anywhere without SJ at any other time. Once, when Sammy asked to use her for a day trip with some friends, SJ refused saying 'you aren't capable.'

"And you think you are?" was Sammy's diplomatic response.

We had decided to spend the day fishing. Joe, who went out in his nephew's boat, knew where cod were to be caught and he was to be our pilot for the day. Down the lough, through the narrows, out over the bar; this was the way to spend a summer day - friends happily working together in harmony. The occasional car could be seen

10

on the coast road, their occupants wasting time on the more mundane things of life as we enjoyed the peace and tranquillity of nature - at one with the elements.

"Get that piggin' dinghy on board!" SJ's roar brought me out of my reverie.

"What are you doing?" he continued as I came back to hoist the dinghy on the stern davits. "We are here to catch fish, not to stand around looking at bloody seagulls."

Arriving at the spot indicated by Joe we cut the engines and the serious business of the day began. Joe was obviously an expert, his tackle far superior to the schoolboy gear used by Steve and myself. Nevertheless it was Steve who landed the first catch of the day, a mackerel, which spurred the rest of us on to greater efforts. The mackerel remained alone in the huge fish box we had optimistically brought along. As the day wore on we decided it was time for some food. The weather had changed a little bit, a breeze from the sea sending short choppy waves in to make it almost impossible to keep the kettle on the cooker. Shelter was needed so that we could enjoy our meal, so we headed behind a nearby island and dropped anchor in its lee.

Mugs of tea to hand - SJ had a glass of rum - we could relax and lie to one another of the fish we had caught in the past. "I remember one time off the Mull of Kintyre." SJ began.

"What boat were you in?" interrupted Joe.

"This one. Why?"

"Oh," said Joe. "I wouldn't fancy going too far in this thing."

SJ was livid. He stood up and towered above Joe, his sixteen stone frame quivering with rage. "You could find yourself in the water if you don't shut your mouth."

Joe stood up too and faced SJ, his nose level with SJ's chest. "Who is going to put me in it?" he asked.

"Me," said SJ "Do you think I couldn't?"

"Not on your best day son." said Joe and he adopted a boxer's pose, fists raised as he did an Ali shuffle on the deck.

"Hey!" shouted Steve. We looked round to where he was peering overboard. "Come here quick."

Fight forgotten we rushed across to see what Steve was pointing at. A huge shoal of fish, each about three feet long was passing under the boat, showing up perfectly against the sandy bottom in the crystal clear waters.

"Mullet," said Joe derisively. "You'll never catch them.

He was right of course but we spent a long time trying, dropping the bait to dangle beguilingly in front of their noses, only to watch as they totally ignored it and swam on. Finally they were all gone and we were left to contemplate what might have been. Despite our failure to catch the mullet we were inspired by them and couldn't wait to get back to some serious fishing. The weather had worsened somewhat back in the open sea and, as soon as the engines were cut, it became very uncomfortable. The Lady Jane lay broadside to the waves, the rocking motion making us all feel decidedly ill.

"We need to anchor," SJ announced. "Then she'll lie into the waves and it will be a lot more comfortable."

"You can't anchor here." said Joe. "The bottom is all very rough rock, it'll be almost impossible to get the anchor up again."

"Well we can't put up with this for much longer," said SJ "Is there anywhere sheltered we can fish?"

"Not if you want to catch cod," was Joe's reply.

"Wait a minute," said SJ "I know the very thing." He started the engines and brought the Lady Jane round into the seas and back towards the entrance to the lough.

"Are we heading back in?" I asked.

"No," was the short reply. Then, a few minutes later, "Go up and fix a rope to the front cleats. One end on each side. It will form a loop over the bows, but keep the rope coiled until I tell you."

Puzzled I went forward and did as I was told, glancing back to see if what I was doing was to SJ's satisfaction.

"What's this for?" asked Steve, abandoning the fishing and coming to join me on the bows.

"I don't know. Unless it is some sort of a sea anchor which he has heard about."

Intent on my task and hanging on to the bucking deck I had not really taken stock of our surroundings. As the

engines slowed I glanced up to see where we were and
then rushed back to the wheelhouse to confront SJ.

"You have got to be kidding." I said.

"Why? What harm can it do?" he replied, concentrat-
ing on the controls. "Now nip out and lasso that bugger."

"No way," I said. "You simply can't do this."

"What's the matter?" asked Joe pushing past me into
the wheelhouse and peering out through the windscreen.

"He only wants to tie up to the Whistler," I said,
expecting some support.

"Good idea," said Joe. "Maybe we can settle down
then and get some serious fishing done."

The Whistler buoy marks the entrance to the lough.
Day and night it guides travellers safely to the lough, its
red and white sphere a welcome sight on the way home.
Now we were going to use it as a glorified mooring.

While SJ held the Lady Jane steady Joe and Steve went
forward to throw the rope over the buoy. My mutiny was
noted but overlooked for the moment. Steve flung the
rope and it sailed over the buoy, sliding down the rounded sides into the water. SJ stopped the engines and we
drifted slowly away from the buoy until the rope held;
then we lay beautifully into the seas, quite comfortable on
our new mooring.

And so back to the fishing. While the others went to it
with enthusiasm I was not content, scanning the sea for
boats, listening to the radio waiting for somebody to come
and arrest us. "Content yourself," said SJ "Nobody even
knows we're here."

Two cod and an hour later I was still looking over my
shoulder; then I saw it, a low, grey, sinister shape materi-
alising from the south. As it got closer I began to make
out details on the structure, like the swept back funnels.
The white markings on the battle grey hull. The tiny figures scurrying about the decks. The guns, pointing sky-
ward, but lowering menacingly as they drew closer.

"SJ," I called.

"What?" he said disinterestedly without looking round.

"I think you had better take a look at this."

SJ sighed, got slowly to his feet and ambled slowly

down the deck to join me at the bows.

"What?" he snapped, then he gazed open mouthed at the battle-ship speeding towards us. "Let that rope go. Quick!" he roared at me as he scrambled for the controls.

With one end of the rope freed we pulled back from the buoy. I gathered up the free end of the rope, trying to pull it through the scuppers and coil it up while crouched below the rails. I popped my head up. The navy ship was getting closer, an officer with a pair of binoculars easily visible on the bridge.

"But how did they know?" asked Steve.

"I'll bet it was that swine in the cabin cruiser who went by. He probably called in to the coastguard and reported us," said SJ, throwing in a few oaths to let us know exactly what he thought of such behaviour.

Ever closer drew the patrol boat. Sailors were at the rail, no doubt preparing to board us and clap us in irons. SJ was reaching for the throttles - whether to make a run for it or give up, I don't know - when the ship veered sharply to the west and headed into the lough, her crew staring disinterestedly at us as she passed.

None of us mentioned the incident as we went home, but SJ got the last word in as usual. "You should have known not to tie up there," he said to me as we landed.

# 3

## OUT FROM KILLYBAY

It was a Saturday afternoon when the phone rang. "Get in here as soon as you can," SJ said. "I have something to show you."

The 'something' was a navigation system. Bits of it were strewn round his kitchen. SJ had an AC/DC converter wired up and was fiddling with the wires.

"There!" he cried triumphantly, as the screen flickered into life. A set of coordinates was displayed on the set. "Is that right?" SJ asked his son Sammy, who was poring over an Ordnance Survey map,

"I don't know," Sammy said. Between us Sammy and I decided that it was far from right - according to the read-out, we were currently about one hundred miles away.

"Where's the instruction book?" I asked.

The manual was found under the packaging on the floor, SJ not being much into the theory side of things. I had a quick read through the book, and then punched some new information into the navigator.

"What was that?" SJ asked suspiciously.

"I was putting in the latitude and longitude of where we are now," I explained.

"That's no piggin' use!" SJ cried. "It's supposed to tell us where we are - not the other way round."

After some explanations, SJ was still far from convinced, so I decided to risk a test.

"If it's working properly," I said, "then by punching this button here, we should get a change in the figures."

I pushed the button and nothing happened. The set should have adjusted our position, and changed the

15

approximate location I had given it to an exact one. SJ was lifting the phone to order the machine to be returned, when Sammy had a brain-wave.

"What about the aerial?" he asked. Sammy took the aerial outside onto the flat roof of the office - and the display obediently changed.

"There you are," I said smugly to SJ. "Your position to the last inch - well, yard or two."

And so I was appointed navigator of the Lady Jane on the spot.

The following morning we all assembled on the quay at Killybay. There was frantic activity as the new navigation system was installed. Eagle Eye, an electrician by trade, was up the mast fitting the aerial; Knot and Sammy drilled holes and fed wires through the wheelhouse; I bolted the display unit above the helmsman's chair.

SJ, a cigarette in one hand and a glass in the other, supervised us all. He was an expert at supervision, was SJ. He would watch until the crucial moment; then, when the sweat was really flowing and a burst finger was throbbing beautifully, he would say, "Don't make a big job out of it, boys."

Exactly on time, all systems were go and we glided majestically across the still, green water from the mooring to the quay. Eagle Eye's wife Mary and the long -suffering spouse of SJ were meeting us for an inaugural cruise. Hampers and baskets were passed on board and off we went, the jealous gaze of the less fortunate land-lubbers following us down the lough.

It was a perfect afternoon. The sea was totally calm; not a ripple marred the mirror-like surface. An occasional seal would pop up to view us with its sad eyes, then disappear again. The tiny green islands were dotted with sheep and cattle, grazing peacefully.

All too soon it was time to turn for home. About four miles from Killybay there was a sudden crack, followed by a lurch to the right. The engines slowed and died as everyone rushed to see what was going on.

"I think we caught a rope back there," SJ said. "The starboard engine has stopped driving." He revved the engine to show us.

"What now?" asked Eagle Eye. "Can you take us in on one engine?"

"Dunno," said SJ. "Let's see." Cautiously, he revved the port engine and, with the wheel almost full lock to port, managed to keep the Lady Jane in a fairly straight line. Mrs SJ and Mary settled back to sleep off their lunch, while the rest of us kept a lookout for any further obstructions.

As it was a calm evening, there seemed to be very little problem for SJ to get us back to Killybay. We were discussing the possible causes and what repairs might be necessary when a sudden scream made us spin round.

"What?" SJ snapped as Mary leapt to her feet, holding her hand to her mouth.

"Look," she yelled and pointed down the galley steps.

We followed her despairing gesture and could see the galley carpet floating back from the steps, revealing an inch of water covering the floor.

"We're all going to die!" wailed Mrs SJ, cowering back in her seat to get away from the water.

"Shut your face!" ordered SJ, as he hoisted himself from his chair and stalked down the wheelhouse to inspect the damage. He gazed at the water for a minute or two without speaking, then made one of those instant diagnoses for which he is justly famous.

"The prop shaft has sheared and has fallen out of the stern tube. That's where the water is getting in. And," he added ominously, "the heavier she gets, the quicker it will come in."

Mary heard the last bit and joined Mrs SJ in wailing and crying.

"Your poor wee children will be orphans." Mrs SJ told Mary in an attempt to calm her down but, surprisingly, it had quite the opposite effect. "And your poor wife and children," she said to me.

"We'll be all right," I told her, trying to keep my voice calm, and thinking of the dinghy tied to our mooring back in Killybay.

SJ took charge. "Get something to block the tube with.

It's about an inch and a half," he told me. "You," he ordered Eagle Eye, "look over the side and check that both pumps are working. If they are, get the pump from the shower and throw it into the galley." Finally he turned to the two women: "Shut up or get up on deck where I can't hear you."

They departed, muttering; Mary to perch nervously on the port rail, while Mrs SJ held grimly to the wheelhouse door preaching doom and gloom. I found a hand-brush and decided that, with a cloth wound round the handle, it should fit the hole. Lying head first down the galley steps, I prised the floorboard up and let it float away. The pressure of the water flooding in made it almost impossible for me to push the handle into the hole, but finally I succeeded.

"Right!" I yelled at SJ. He started the engine and we

felt our way back towards safety.

The Lady Jane was acquiring a definite list.  From lying on the steps I was now almost lying on the wall.  Mrs SJ was having difficulty hanging onto the wheelhouse door. "We're going to turn over!" she wailed.

"Is it any wonder with the weight of you?" SJ snapped. "Get over to the other side and she'll probably right herself."

Eagle Eye helped Mrs SJ across to the port rail, but it did not make any difference.

"Couldn't you run into that island?" I heard her shout. "Then we could all jump off."

Sammy had been on the radio trying to summon help and the first volunteer arrived as we rounded the town rock at Killybay.

"How may we be of assistance?" a loudspeaker squawked.

"Tell him we're home now and to **** off," SJ barked.

Sammy thanked the yacht for the offer, and asked where we might get a mains pump.  This was duly waiting when we tied up at the quay, and the Lady Jane was soon righted and looking her old self.  The two ladies left in a huff.

"Never again," said Mrs SJ, shaking her head.

"Do you think we'd ask you?" SJ replied.

# 4

## KILLYBAY TO PORT ERIN

Following our recent disaster, a new prop shaft had been made in SJ's workshop and it together with a new propeller, had already been fitted. There were no signs of any problems as we set sail that Friday afternoon.

A check at the Whistler Buoy showed that the navigator was exactly right. Heartened by this, I laid in a course for the Isle of Man and we were on our way. Course, speed, ETA, even the corrections we needed to make - these were now all laid out before us in a beautiful green, so navigation was a relatively simple matter. Sammy, SJ's son, decided that the radar equipment was in the wrong place and fetched the tool kit to move it.

"If it's not broke yet, don't fix it," commented SJ, so Sammy left it alone.

The weather was very kind to us that early summer evening. A sea of glass was disturbed only by the occasional seagull, joined by Manx shearwaters as we neared our destination. SJ called me forward from the galley when we were still about an hour from land. "What's that noise?" he asked.

I listened hard. "What noise?" I said at last.

"There's something not right," SJ insisted. "Get Sammy and have a look at that stern tube."

Sammy and I lifted the boards and examined the shaft where it disappeared into the stern tube. There was a tiny weep of water there, but nothing to worry about. We greased the gland and went back to report to the skipper.

"I still don't like it," he said. " Can't you hear it?" When we had all replied in the negative, SJ announced, "You're

all deaf," and settled back smugly, waiting to prove us wrong.

Half and hour later we all knew something was wrong. First the cups and glasses in the galley started to rattle, gently at first then with an increasing and irritating regularity. Next, we could feel the drubbing beneath our feet.

SJ reduced the revs, first to one thousand eight hundred, then to one thousand two hundred, then to one thousand. Each time the vibration eased for a few minutes, only to start up again.

The Calf of Man was dead ahead; the gap between it and the main island was our passage through, and Douglas our final destination. A breeze had sprung up as we neared the land, and this increased in strength the closer we got.

"Don't you think we should maybe put in to Port Erin?" I asked, "just to be on the safe side." I had been reading up on Calf Sound - where we were now headed - and did not fancy going through it on one engine.

"Not at all," SJ said. "If we keep the revs down Lady Jane will be all right. Anyway I've been to Port Erin, there's nowhere to tie up. We'd have to lie at a mooring and go in and out in the dinghy."

He was starting to say something else when I saw him swallow hard, his eyes opening wider and wider as he stared ahead. When the tide and the wind are opposed to one another, as was the case tonight, Calf Sound is not a place for the faint-hearted. A curtain of seething white water was drawn across the whole sound, barring our passage and obscuring the open sea beyond.

"Well, Port Erin here we come," said SJ spinning the wheel.

Food had not been top of my list of priorities for the past few hours but, as safety neared, I nipped back to put on the kettle. We had come up the coast past Heifer Rock and the magnificent entrance to Port Erin was opening up for us, so a cup of tea seemed in order."Where are you going?" I asked SJ as I came back up to the wheelhouse.

"Straight in," he replied confidently.

"Don't you see that buoy?" I asked, pointing out a large

green object away to our left.

"That!" SJ replied contemptuously. "That's only for big ships."

Eagle Eye was at the bows, getting ready to tie up, when we saw him jump up and down in some distress. "What the **** is wrong with him?" SJ asked.

"Rocks! ROCKS!" The words came floating back. We were almost totally surrounded by beautifully quarried stone, piled up haphazardly to catch the unwary - or plain stupid.

The good citizens of Port Erin had, about a hundred years before, decided to build themselves a new break-water. The first big storm had demolished their handi-work however, so they stuck a marker on it, and left it as a monument to man's feebleness against the elements.

SJ threw both throttles into reverse. The screws bit and slowly we backed out of that graveyard, Eagle Eye and Sammy running back and forth yelling instructions.

It was the final straw, as far as the shaft was concerned; with a bang, the coupling at the gearbox parted company with the shaft, and we were left with one engine. SJ had fitted collars on the shafts this time, so there was no danger of our losing one, but steerage was a problem.

The Lady Jane described a huge circle into Port Erin's natural harbour and, despite our best efforts, headed out again. Several attempts later, the remaining engine was killed and we had a council of war.

"We could jockey back and forward," Sammy suggested, "until we are as close as possible to that visitor's mooring. Then somebody could take a rope to it in the dinghy."

That was more or less agreed upon and we went back to our zigzag course. Sammy and Eagle Eye prepared and launched the dinghy, and got the outboard running. I had read an article about steering a disabled yacht with a dinghy so I explained this to Sammy and we decided to give it a try.

The painter was tied fairly tightly to the Lady Jane quite far forward on the starboard side, a longer stern line was then attached, allowing the back of the dinghy to swing away. When the outboard was started, the dinghy

nosed into the Lady Jane, ropes tightening to maximum as Sammy increased the revs.

It might have worked.

SJ stuck his head out of the wheelhouse door. "What are you doing?" he demanded.

I started to explain but he cut me short.

"Let her go," he ordered Eagle Eye, who let go; first the bow line then, by pulling the slip knot, the stern.

Like a scalded cat, the dinghy skittered off across the bay. Sammy, taken completely by surprise, tumbled into the bottom of the boat, legs waving furiously as he tried to get up. On full revs the dinghy careered to the end of its rope, like an upside down turtle on waterskis. Once out of free rope it swung in a huge arc, disappearing from view behind the wheelhouse to re-emerge at the stern.

Round she went again, Sammy still trying valiantly to regain control - or at least an upright position.

The port engine's note deepened, then died - it had picked up the rope from the dinghy. Powerless, the tide and wind carried us past the new breakwater, past the jetty, onto the beach.

We threw out the anchor, of course, but the sandy bottom provided no purchase until it was too late.

# 5

## AT PORT ERIN

We were heading for the sandy beach of Port Erin and there was very little we could do about it.

Eagle Eye threw the anchor overboard and locked the winch. The anchor bounced ineffectually across the hard sand of the bottom.

"More chain! More chain!" shouted SJ.

We let out more chain and the anchor bit just as we grounded. Without the ability to swing to the anchor the Lady Jane was steadily rocked back and forth, lying hull-on to the waves, the anchor chain eating greedily at the forepeak sheeting. Sammy had pulled himself and the dinghy back alongside and he clambered aboard to join us. SJ glared wildly round, looking for inspiration.

"Join all the rope on board together and take it across to the harbour wall," he shouted above the crash of the waves. Sammy and I leapt overboard - up to our waists - with the first rope, while SJ and Eagle Eye frantically tied more lengths together. Up onto the beach we charged, Sammy carrying the rope, while I lifted it over the various craft lying stranded.

A sizeable crowd had gathered on the pier to watch the fun, and one old salt took charge immediately. He grabbed the rope from Sammy, wound it round a steel bollard and organised the rabble into a thirty strong tug-of-war team. Slowly, inch by agonising inch, Lady Jane's head came round.

"The tide's going out," one helpful soul advised. "You're wasting your time."

A boat came into sight round the harbour wall. It had

taken a load of sightseers to Calf Island and was return-
ing them to terra firma. The skipper quickly assessed the
situation and, having dropped his passengers, backed his
craft in towards the Lady Jane on the beach. "Hold
tight!" the beach-master cried. "She's not off yet."

Sammy put his head on one side, listening. "That's a
Gardner. She should soon have us off," he said.

"What's a gardener got to do with anything?" I
snapped, muscles aching. "Do you want to plant flowers
on the bloody thing?"

"A Gardner. The engine on that boat is a Gardner."

The Gardner snarled and smoked and pulled the Lady
Jane off the beach.

"Can you dry out?" the beach-master enquired of me.
When I said that we could not he waved to the skipper of
the tug that he should take the Lady Jane out to the
breakwater. "Right," he said, turning to the crowd: "We'll
have to go down and pull her in to the breakwater." Most
of the team had already figured that out, however, and
had made themselves scarce: they had enough blisters for
the one day.

Lashed fore and aft to the breakwater we had a quick
meal, then ripped up the floorboards to assess the damage.
The rubber couplings between the gearbox and the shaft
had broken, the size of the ends indicating that they had
taken a lot of abuse before shearing off.

I went off to the shops to stock up for what looked like
an extended stay in Port Erin. On my return to the Lady
Jane there was a new development. Liverpool University
has a marine research centre based in Port Erin and SJ
had commandeered one of its divers to carry out an
underwater assessment of the damage. We leaned anxiously over the side, waiting.

"One of the rudders is bent quite badly," the diver
announced on surfacing, "and one of the props has a
piece doubled over."

"Could you tie a rope to the rudder?" SJ asked. "We
can then drop it out from up here and pull it aboard."

The diver gave the okay sign, and popped out of sight
with the rope Sammy had passed to him. Eagle Eye and I

rushed below, flung seats and carpets aside and uncoupled the steering rudder shaft. Meanwhile SJ had given the diver a pair of vice grips and asked him to straighten the propeller.

Everything was ready. I tapped the rudder shaft and it dropped out and onto the bottom. We pulled it up and examined it. Where the blade met the shaft it was bent over to an angle of about forty degrees. The sledge-hammer failed to make any impression on it, so Eagle Eye and Sammy were despatched to find something that would. The diver prepared to leave.

"Can't you stay till they get back?" SJ asked. It seemed that the diver, Nigel, could wait for a while, but he had to examine nets in the afternoon and must be back by then.

Sammy and Eagle Eye charged up to the town carrying the damaged rudder between them. Every time they met someone who looked like a local, they asked where they might find a press but nobody knew. Sammy flagged down a tractor in the middle of the town - a farmer ought to know the local repair shops if anyone did. He did, but suggested that the weight of his tractor might straighten the shaft.

Sammy laid the shaft down in the road and the farmer reversed his tractor onto it. The rudder was too hard to respond to this type of treatment, however, and skidded away from the tractor wheel.

Eagle Eye spotted the railway line and suggested wedging the rudder under it. The tractor was just about to reverse onto the rudder again when a car screeched to a halt, driven by a local railway employee. He did not seem very pleased at this misuse of a tourist attraction and only the presence of the farmer prevented him from calling the police. A taxi eventually took them to an engineering works suggested by the farmer and a quick push with a hydraulic press was all that was required to restore the rudder to its full efficiency.

Back at the breakwater SJ and I had to work very hard to keep our captive diver from escaping. I made tea and SJ tried offering whisky. When this failed he offered that other old standby - money.

Nigel insisted that he couldn't take pay but a couple of tenners was shoved into his diving suit anyway.

A second diver appeared, looking for the first, so SJ promptly press-ganged him as well. A little more time passed and the divers' boatman turned up; the same man who had pulled us off the day before. SJ offered payment - which was refused quite brusquely. It began to look as if we might lose our divers. Casually I asked the boatman if he had a Gardner in his boat.

"How do you know that?" he asked.

"Oh, by the sound of it," I replied modestly.

His attitude changed right away. While SJ and the boatman avidly discussed the workings of marine engines, I sidled back, trying not to get involved in the conversation, which would reveal me as a fraud.

Just as the conversation was beginning to flag and the boatman was looking at his watch, Sammy and Eagle Eye returned with the straightened rudder. Nigel and his colleague dutifully went back into the water and we lowered the rudder down to them. There was much churning of mud and many bangs on the hull, but eventually the shaft of the rudder came poking back through its hole and we tightened the nuts.

"I wonder how long we're going to be stuck in this God-forsaken hole?" asked Sammy as we surveyed the scene from the breakwater that evening.

"Look on the bright side," Eagle Eye said. "The holiday-makers up there are paying good money to stay in Port Erin."

# 6

## MAROONED

Port Erin breakwater has several disadvantages as an overnight berth. We were just about to drop off to sleep that night when we discovered the first of them. The peace and calm of our little haven was disturbed by a grating from the bows.

"What the hell is that?" shouted Eagle Eye from the head.

"We're aground!" yelled Sammy and, half-asleep, he grabbed a life-jacket and headed for the deck - re-living his nightmare of that afternoon.

"Naw," SJ grunted from his double berth in the galley. "We need to move her back a bit. As the tide goes out we're going aground at the bows. Hop out and shift her."

Eagle Eye and I duly went out into the chill night air and heaved and pulled until the Lady Jane was safely and snugly lying in deep water once again.

And so to bed. I was awakened - sometime in the middle of the night - by SJ roaring. "Robert! Eagle Eye! Sammy! What the hell are you doing?"

Eagle Eye and I arrived from our cabins at the same time. Sammy, well used to SJ shouting at any time of the day or night, was curled up asleep on the wheelhouse seats a happy smile playing over his lips. I don't know what he was dreaming about but it was not Port Erin.

"What's up?" Eagle Eye and I both gasped at the same time.

"We are," SJ announced. "Up on top of the wall. When you two clowns moved her last night you must have moved her too far back. When the tide came in

again it lifted us onto the top of the breakwater."

Eagle Eye and I staggered outside. I tried to waken Sammy on the way past but it was no use. He just grabbed my hand, smiled even wider and murmured "Oh yes, darling. Yes."

I beat a hasty retreat and joined Eagle Eye on the breakwater. The tide was covering the lower end of the wall, over which the stern of the Lady Jane was bounced with each wave. What's more the rope securing us to said breakwater was a good two feet underwater. Eagle Eye stuck one bare foot into the cold tide then turned to me: "Toss you for it," he offered.

SJ stuck his head out of the wheelhouse door. "What are you doing?"

"We have to untie her so we can move her up." I volunteered.

"So?"

"So somebody is going to have to get wet," I snapped back. "I don't suppose it's going to be you?"

"There's more than one end to a piece of rope," SJ said and disappeared back to his berth.

Eagle Eye and I looked at one another for a minute or two. "Oh," I finally said lamely, and went on board to let go the aft mooring.

Port Erin breakwater is just that - a breakwater, not a harbour wall. At high tide the lower end of the wall is completely submerged, and at low tide the top end is left high and dry. For the remainder of our stay we had to move the Lady Jane with every high and low tide. Back and forward. Back and forward.

We awakened to a scene of utter chaos. Floorboards were propped against the edges of seats, leaving a lattice-work of struts across which we had to perform a tightrope act to get from one end of the boat to the other.

Breakfast over we stripped the coupling between engine and gearbox to find that the rubber joints were completely wrecked.

"Ring Stuarty," SJ ordered me.

"Who's Stuarty?" I asked.

Stuarty, it seemed, was the agent for Borg-Warner

gearboxes and could be relied on to pull us out of a hole at any time of the day or night.

"But it's Sunday," I protested, "I can't ring somebody on a Sunday morning about spare parts."

"Course you can," said SJ confidently. "Stuarty won't mind. If he does you tell him from me to 'xxxxxxxxxxxxxx'" Here followed a set of instructions which were physically impossible and morally unacceptable.

Armed with his phone number and a pile of change I set out to phone Stuarty. The Isle of Man is a funny place - the streets are free of rubbish and the phones work. As I waited for Stuarty to answer the phone I wondered how I would feel if I was answering the phone at seven o'clock on a Sunday morning to deal with a business call.

Stuarty was not impressed. "Do you know what time it is?" he practically yelled down the phone.

I did but, surmising that it was probably a rhetorical question, I refrained from giving it to him; instead I told him why I was ringing. It is strange but, despite his manner, people seem to go out of their way for SJ. If I had been ringing for myself Stuarty would probably have told me to ring on Monday and hung up. As it was he said: "Oh, SJ, hang on until I get a pen."

Having taken the details Stuarty promised to have the parts sent as soon as possible - Post Restante Port Erin - and went back to whatever it was he had been doing.

There was nothing much we could do without parts so Sammy, Eagle Eye and I decided to see the sights of Port Erin. SJ, as always, declined our offer to come ashore; on all the trips we made he never set a foot on dry land while we were on foreign shores - so to speak.

Coming back from an exciting afternoon viewing the railway museum and the aquarium, we found SJ had company. The man who ran one of the boats taking trippers from the harbour had dropped in. "About time too," SJ greeted us. He shoved some money forward. "Here. Nip out and get us another bottle." I looked round me to see who he was talking to but the other pair had disappeared.

The other man protested but SJ insisted. "One more will do you no harm."

The breakwater in Port Erin is set half-way down a long dead-end road from the town. There is a pub on this road, near the Raglan Pier, but it was closed so I had to trek into the town itself. Hot, sticky and footsore I headed back. The tide was coming in and a small queue was forming beside a blackboard on the pier. 'Visit the bird sanctuary on Calf Island,' it announced. 'Next trip 6-00 PM.'

SJ did not thank me for my efforts. "Where did you go for this? The distillery?" he snapped, and snatching the bottle from me added: "Any change?"

Back out on the breakwater I sat with Eagle Eye and Sammy admiring the view. Half an hour passed, then we were hailed by a small man wearing a peaked cap from the road. "Hello!"

We wandered down to see what he wanted. "Have you seen Tom?" he asked and went on to describe the man sitting on the Lady Jane with SJ. He took the news rather badly. "We have a bloody boat to take out," he cried. "That man hasn't touched a drink in five years. Why did he have to start today?"

We all looked into the Lady Jane but it was too late: Tom was trying to light a cigarette, tip end out. "If he can't find the end of a cigarette," said Eagle Eye, "He will hardly be able to find Calf Island."

Leaving the drinkers to it we all trudged off to the pier. "Is the boat nearly ready to go?" a fat matron demanded.

"Sorry," our companion said as he hurried past, "technical problems."

"Can't you take her out?" Sammy asked when we were on board - peering into the engine compartment to mollify the increasingly irate trippers.

"I suppose so," came the reply. "But I need an engineer - for insurance purposes."

"Sammy is the best there is," volunteered Eagle Eye.

"Has he got a ticket?" was the next question.

"No. But I have," said Eagle Eye. (So he had. As part of his job Eagle Eye repaired ship's electrics and this often meant he had to sail with the vessel.)

"..And to our left, we can see a fine example of traditional 'Isle of Man' folk dancing

We were signed on. Eagle Eye and Sammy as the combined engineer, me as money-collector. Not a minute too soon. A stone whizzed past my ear. I looked up; the culprit, about ten years old, stared back unrepentant. "Are you gonna keep us standin 'ere all day?" he demanded.

All aboard and we set sail for Calf Island. As we passed the breakwater a lone figure detached itself from the Lady Jane and staggered to the end of the wall. I waved. "Here. Where do you think you are going with my bloody boat?" The drink may have affected his balance but not his lungs. There followed a string of oaths which would have been admired in any port in the world. The fat lady turned to me. "What did he say?" she asked.

"Just wishing us Bon Voyage in Manx," I replied waving to Tom. The rest of the party joined in, waving merrily as we chugged past the breakwater. This sent

Tom into a fit of rage;  he danced up and down on the wall, waving his fists and screaming obscenities.  In his anger Tom forgot where the end of the wall was.  He danced over the end and into the water.  "Shouldn't we go back and rescue him?"  asked Sammy anxiously.

"Safer not,"  said the stand-in skipper as he headed out to sea.

# 7

## KILLYBAY TO PORTPATRICK

Finally we had managed to arrange a whole week away. Scotland was selected as the lucky venue for our holiday.

Crew members were in short supply - most of them had to work, so they said. Old Bob was chosen as the cook from a short-list of one. He, together with the skipper SJ, his son Sammy and myself, made up the ship's complement.

Old Bob was a good choice as cook; as well as being available, he had no immediate family - apart from a budgie - to worry about him. He generally did as he was told, unless he didn't want to. There were only two draw-backs to Old Bob's appointment: firstly, he couldn't cook; secondly, he was quite mad.

In quiet moments, when one was completely relaxed and not expecting it, he would suddenly yelp like a dog, or go "YIP" at the top of his voice. Whoever was beside him, after they had recovered from the shock, would turn towards him, waiting for something further, but Bob would give no indication that anything had happened. Gaze at him too long and he would ask sharply: "What?"

Another of Old Bob's little foibles was to say: "It's a hard life without a wife, but a worse life with one." Hearing it the first time was quite amusing, but hearing it every fifteen minutes was a bit much.

Everything had been seen to. Life-jackets were checked and Old Bob was shown how to put his on. The engines had been given a full service the weekend before. All the equipment was thoroughly gone over, even before we let go the mooring. I had listened to the forecast that

morning and we listened again on the RT on our way
down the lough to the open sea.

"Force two to three," Sammy said. "That doesn't sound
too bad. We should have a nice, quiet crossing."

The bar was a little bit lumpy but, once in the bay,
Sammy's prediction seemed to be coming true. Three
hours was a reasonable passage time across the North
Channel and we discussed the possibility of pressing on a
little bit further than we had planned that day. There
seemed to be more small craft than usual requesting
weather reports from the Coastguard. "Force two to
three," they were all being told.

"Day trippers!" Sammy snorted. "Could they not listen
to the BBC like the rest of us?"

"YIP!" shouted Old Bob.

An hour out from the bar and things were not looking
so rosy. The sea was a nasty grey colour, coming at us
from all directions. SJ was forced to disengage the auto-
matic pilot to avoid the worst of the waves. Up ahead we
could see a lot of white water, while waves were beginning
to break over the bows. Yet again the Coastguard, in a
bored voice, repeated the forecast.

"Must be a localised thing," I said.

"If we head south a bit we should get a quieter ride," SJ
said. "Can you set a new course once we get closer to the
Scottish coast?"

"Oh, aye," I said confidently. "No problems."

The weather got steadily worse. The wipers were on
full speed but, even so, the helmsman had to stand peering out ahead. SJ soon tired of this and handed over to
Sammy. I was hanging on to the chart table for all I was
fit, while Bob stretched out on the seat behind me, his
head resting on the box of provisions we had brought
with us.

Every time Sammy tried to bring the Lady Jane on to a
more northerly heading it became almost impossible to
hang on. Still the radio droned on: "Irish Sea. Southerly
Force two to three."

SJ didn't let him finish: "Get that ill-begotten son of a
***** on the radio and tell him to come out here and see

what it's like for himself." Too late. Somebody was already on: they had lost their mast and required immediate assistance.

Listening to the rescue details passed the time for us and we hung on grimly and shared in the drama. We heard that a line had just been passed to the stricken yacht when a particularly nasty sea caught us, tipping the Lady Jane right over so that the port windows dipped under the water. Old Bob fell from one seat to the other, without touching the six feet of carpet which lay in between. The box of groceries came after him, and he struggled upright with broken eggs and milk streaming down his face.

It took quite a while to get Bob cleaned up and wedged into a safe seat. The mess on the floor and the seats I left for a quieter time.

Back beside Sammy at the wheel, I noted down the details from the navigator, then tried to pencil in our position on the chart. We were about twenty miles north of Glasgow. I glanced wildly through the windows, but, as there were no houses about, I took a deep breath and tried, again.

"Six," I muttered under my breath, punching the button. "Position." Still the same - on dry land. "Course and speed made good." I punched that up next. Even worse, we were heading south west - that did not make any sense at all. "What-ah-I mean, did you change course lately?" I asked Sammy.

"Not really," he said "When Old Bob fell off the seat I must have let her go a bit. But when I noticed I brought her back on course. See." He pointed to the navigator. The indicator showed that we were following the pro-grammed course to the yard - heading straight through Glasgow towards Portpatrick. "It's a bit easier going now, anyway," Sammy observed.

"Of course it is," I snapped back. "We are going in the wrong flaming direction, that's why. Did you notice any-thing happening with the navigator?"

"Aye," Sammy said. "When we hit that big wave the screen went blank. Only for a second, like. I was going to call you, but it came back on almost immediately. Is it important?"

It had been almost an hour since I had last penciled in our position. Trying not to be sick and hanging on had occupied most of my attention. We could be almost any-where. With the change of course we might even be back to where the navigator had gone on the blink.

I made a finely judged approximation of our present position, taking into account wind, tides, speed, last known position and time elapsed - a very rough guess, in other words.

Having fed this information into the navigator we got a new heading and brought the Lady Jane about onto it. We glanced round nervously, waiting for an explosion from SJ but he was just staring ahead, probably praying for the ordeal to be over.

"Where are we headed now?" Sammy asked. He had more confidence in my skills than me.

"Scotland," I said firmly. Adding under my breath, "I hope,"

On we plunged, with waves breaking over us. The day drew to a close, darkness sneaking in from all sides. I was spelling Sammy at the wheel when he called out: "There's a light up ahead." We counted the flashes, then timed them.

"It's the Mull of Galloway," I said, consulting the almanac. "We'll turn left," There are no ports or starboards in a crisis.

Slowly we crawled up the rocky coast. Portpatrick was the first - the only - port we could find shelter in. I put Sammy back on the wheel and read out all the information on the entrance to him. The lights were very well described - unfortunately they were totally obscured by the street lighting beyond them, but we finally made it into the inner harbour.

I was tying up, beside the dismasted yacht, when a holiday-maker called down to me. "Rough crossing?"

"Not too bad," I nonchalantly replied.

"YIP!" Old Bob cried weakly from below.

# 8

## PORTPATRICK TO KILLYBAY

Once safely in Portpatrick we were able to relax and enjoy our holiday. Bob decided to cook a meal but, as the baked beans were added to the sausages in the pan, Sammy and I rejected the offering and headed ashore.

There is a delightful little cafe not far from the harbour and here we dined in a civilised manner, missing neither Bob's yelps nor SJ's oaths. Back to the ship. Bob had kindly kept us some food, but it had not improved with the keeping so again we declined. SJ was looking a little green round the gills and his plate was only half empty so perhaps it was for the best.

A bit of a clean up was needed. There were broken eggs, pieces of broken glass, all sorts lying about. I got the brush and shovel out and was making a start when Sammy pushed me out of the way. "That's an old-fashioned way to do it," he said, producing a vacuum cleaner from the front cabin. Sammy had 'borrowed' his mother's new cleaner without telling her about it. We made lots of new friends as we revved the port engine up to 1500 rpm to get the correct frequency for the mains generator.

Chores done we settled back for a chat; Sammy and I with a cup of tea, Bob with a beer and SJ with the customary glass of rum.

"This takes me back," said old Bob. "During the war I sailed round the Mediterranean in a commandeered Italian torpedo boat." He went on to describe his wartime adventures, Sammy and I almost dropping off to sleep, SJ nodding encouragement between swallows.

"There was a budgie on the boat," said Bob nostalgically.

"A lovely wee thing. Must have been the captain's." He stopped, a look of horror coming over his face. "Oh God!" he cried. "The poor wee thing. It will have starved to death by now."

"Don't worry about it," said SJ. "After forty odd years its nearly bound to be dead anyway."

"Not that budgie," said old Bob. "My budgie. I forgot to tell Mrs Gordon I was going away."

Sammy and I were sent to phone Mrs Gordon; One-thirty in the morning and Bob couldn't remember her telephone number or her proper address. "It's just round the corner from my house," he explained helpfully.

Directory enquiries were quite helpful too. "Just round the corner from where?. We need an address pal," the operator exclaimed and disconnected. So much for privatisation.

"I can ring my Mum in the morning and get her to go round," Sammy told Bob when we got back on board. "Nothing to worry about."

The next morning we woke to find old Bob haggard and worn, walking the deck. "There's only one key," he exclaimed, grabbing SJ by the arm. "We'll have to go home."

So it was decided, our week long holiday was being cut to two days because of a hungry budgie.

"And if I know him," said Sammy (meaning his father - SJ) "He will have me back working tomorrow morning." So he did too.

After a cold breakfast - Bob was too upset to cook - we cast off and manouvered our way out of the crowded inner harbour. It was a beautiful morning and, as we got far enough into the open sea to see past Corsewall Point, Sammy and I gazed longingly towards Ailsa Craig and beyond where we should have been heading.

"Don't you think we could still go?" Sammy asked SJ.

"And leave that poor wee bird to starve?" said SJ. "Shame on you."

"What about the radio?" I asked. "We could call home and see if your wife would nip round to Mrs Gordon's. Maybe Bob has left a window open or something."

I got onto the R.T. and called Portpatrick Radio. When we got through Mrs SJ was not in and we could only leave a message for her to call back as soon as possible.

The morning wore on. Already Ailsa Craig was fading from view behind, the rock slowly slipping further into the misty sea with every passing minute.

The radio squawked into life. We had our link call from Mrs SJ. "Can you go to Mrs Gordon's and see if you can get her to feed Bob's budgie. Over."

"Feed Bob's budgie over where?"

"Not over anywhere. We just want Mrs Gordon to feed the budgie. Over."

"Over in Bob's house, or over in Mrs Gordon's house?"

I gave up on the overs. "We just want it fed. Okay?"

"Okay." Mrs SJ seemed to have got the message. "So Mrs Gordon is to feed the budgie over in Bob's house?"

"Give me that bloody thing." SJ snatched the microphone out of my hand and roared into it. "Listen, you stupid woman, just get the budgie fed. Right?"

"Okay, okay. Keep your hair on. Has Mrs Gordon got a key?"

"If Mrs Gordon had a key she would know she had to feed the budgie and I would not be wasting my time talking to you."

"Well how is she going to get in then?"

SJ, never a patient man at the best of times was beginning to show signs of apoplexy. "Break the door down. Call the fire brigade. I don't know how you are going to get in. Just get in."

The call was ended. We cruised on in silence for a few minutes. Sammy was the first to speak. "We could have bought him ten budgies for the price of that phone call."

SJ - probably the most mercenary man I have ever met - said: "You can't put a value on everything you know."

Another hour passed. The coast was getting closer. Pleasure craft were shooting out from all the small harbours, waterskiing, cruising, sailing - people making the most of the fine weather and the calm seas to enjoy their holidays - as we should have been doing on the other side of the Irish Sea.

Sammy and I were both dressed in our best leisure clothes. It looked as if we were actually going to finish a cruise looking like pleasure sailors rather than grease monkeys off a coaler. SJ had other ideas however. "Have a look at the stern glands," he ordered.

We dutifully pulled up the boards in the galley and checked the glands. A tiny weep at one was soon cured with a squirt of the grease gun. Sammy wiped his hands down his white trousers. Already the crew of the Lady Jane was starting to look more normal. A quick check of the engine-oil levels gave me a pair of dirty trousers too, and a bloody finger where Sammy dropped a floorboard on it.

We sailed into the lough. Five miles to go to Killybay and home, our long awaited cruise to the Western Isles postponed for another year.

The radio operator was back on. "Link call for the Lady Jane."

Mrs SJ came on the line. "I know what you were talking about now. Over. Oh, wait a minute. Knot was telling me about the radio. Your turn. I mean over."

"What about Bob's house? Were you able to get in? Over."

"No. All the windows were closed and the doors were locked. It's like a bank. Over."

"Well could you see the budgie through any of the windows? Is it all right?"

"What? Sorry. I was trying to talk while you were talking." There was a pause. "Hello are you still there? I mean over. I can't get the hang of this thing at all."

I tried again. "Is Bob's budgie all right?"

"Yes it's fine. Over. You forgot to say over the last time. Over."

"How do you know the budgie is okay? Over."

"Well Mrs Gordon says it is alright and she has a budgie of her own." There was a long pause, then "Over."

"Has Mrs Gordon seen the budgie then? Over."

"Yes of course. Bob left it with her the night before you sailed. Over."

# 9

## PORT ST MARY

It had been an uneventful journey so far. Knot, SJ and myself were the only ones on board the Lady Jane that day. We were heading for Douglas, Isle of Man. This was our third or fourth attempt to reach Douglas - numerous adventures having kept us away before - and it looked as if we might succeed this time.

We sailed through a beautifully calm Calf Sound, Manx shearwaters and various gulls dropping noiselessly from the sheer cliffs. After rounding Spanish head, straight across the bay, was a little headland - Scarlett Point. "Keep well outside that," I advised SJ. "Then round Langness and it's a fairly straight run into Douglas."

"Where's that?" asked Knot, pointing to a huddle of houses to our left clinging grimly to the hillside.

"Port St Mary," I replied. "Do you want to have a look?"

"No way!" said SJ forcefully. "We are going the whole way to Douglas this time if it kills us. Anyway, there's nothing in there. A few hotels, half a dozen pubs, not worth the effort."

At the mention of pubs Knot turned around and looked at Port St Mary as we got farther away. "Looks like a nice place," he said longingly. This was a dry trip. I had insisted that, as there were only three of us going, every-one had to be sober - for the sailing anyway. SJ had, too easily, agreed, so when he gave me his bag to put in the car I took the bottle out of it and hid it under the back seat. He had gone into his cabin just after we sailed, called his wife a few choice names and come out again.

44

Being a perfect gentleman, I said nothing.

In the middle of the bay it got a little bit rough. The waves, increasing all the time, were sweeping in from the open sea and catching us amidships, rolling us back and forward. SJ put his cigarette out and opened the door. Knot sidled up alongside him to catch the breeze. The rolling got worse. SJ took his glasses off and wiped his forehead, leaning further out of the open door to take advantage of the fresh air. A bigger wave struck. SJ was thrown back into his seat, feet in the air. Then, as the Lady Jane slid down the other side of the wave, he was catapulted out through the open door to land head first on the steel deck. Knot managed to grab SJ by the feet before he could complete his forward roll into the sea. "Good job he landed on his head," Knot said later. "Otherwise he might have been hurt."

We pulled the, almost, comatose SJ back into the wheelhouse and laid him out on the floor. "We'll have to put into Port St Mary now," Knot said, spinning the wheel. "That man needs a doctor."

"No doctors," groaned SJ from the floor, raising himself on his elbow.

"Well a brandy then."

"Oh. Okay then," said SJ, lying down again.

The rolling was getting worse as we headed back across the open bay towards Port St Mary. Knot had never been sober, or sane, enough to be allowed to take the wheel before so he was enjoying himself enormously.

The port engine surged, then slowly died. I leaned across Knot and pushed both throttles to neutral.

Knot and I were not qualified to decide what was wrong. I said it was fuel, but the fuel guage said there was plenty. SJ, semi-conscious on the floor, gave us the answer. "The way she was lying coming across the bay has drained the fuel out of one tank into the other - they are connected with a two inch pipe - and the engine has air-locked. You'll have to try and keep her into the waves and bleed the fuel system."

Before we could bleed the fuel system we had to lift the floorboards, and before we could lift the floorboards we had to lift SJ. After a lot of shoving and heaving we had him trailed sufficiently to one side to allow us to get at the injector pump.

As Knot sweated, pumped and cursed I tried to hold the Lady Jane into the sea with our one engine. Finally he roared at me, "Give it a try." The engine coughed, spluttered and roared into life. Fresh from his triumph Knot shoved me out of the helmsman's chair and headed into port.

"Don't!" came weakly from behind us.

Crazed with the power of command Knot flung orders at me. "See what's wrong with him, then get out on deck and prepare to tie up. You'll need to get some of those fender things ready too."

"What did you say?" I asked SJ, who was trying to struggle to his feet, blood trickling down his forehead and dripping off an eyebrow.

He gripped my arm, shaking it to emphasise his words. "Do not let Knot take this boat in." He sank slowly back into a seat then started forward again. "Remember what happened in Portrush." I had never heard of anything happening to Knot, or anyone else, in Portrush, but it sounded pretty ominous so I rushed back up the wheelhouse.

"Well what did he want?" Knot enquired crisply, as befitted the acting captain.

"Em. Ah. Well he said that, as I had more experience like, that I should.... well, that I should take her in."

"Balls," was Knot's considered reply. "Now go and get those ropes ready."

The harbour wall was getting closer so I went on deck to get ready to tie up. Our speed was not being reduced so I stuck my head round the door. "Going a wee bit too fast?" I asked Knot.

"Not at all," he said confidently, but his right hand reached towards the throttles. The harbour was rushing towards us now. Knot reduced the revs by a mere fraction. We shot behind the protecting wall of the outer pier, past a trawler whose two crewmen, working on deck, rushed to the rail to see where the fire was.

"SLOW DOWN!" I roared at Knot. Obediently he pulled the throttles full back into reverse. Still the slipway at the end of the harbour came towards us. Knot stood up and pushed past me. "You can take her in," he said and went to stand in the bows.

Gradually the screws bit and the Lady Jane slowed, stopped and, as I reduced the engine speed, backed perfectly in beside the trawler.

Knot went off to get a bottle of medicinal brandy almost before we were tied up. The two trawlermen, when they heard of our plight, were quite sympathetic, even offering the use of a car to take SJ to hospital. "Once I get my brandy I'll be alright," SJ said, mopping the blood out of his eyes.

The brandy was a long time in coming. Half an hour had passed so I asked one of the seamen how far it was to the nearest pub. "About a hundred yards," he said, so we knew Knot had gone A.W.O.L. I went to get the brandy myself. As I went into the first pub I sensed something was wrong. The overturned tables and broken chairs sort of gave it away. Nevertheless I bravely pressed on with my mission. "A bottle of brandy please," I told the barman.

He turned to the shelf then turned back again. "Here, are you Irish?" he asked with a less than welcoming look.

"Gee buddy I only came in for a bottle of god-damned cognac."

Knot arrived back on board about four hours later. He ate six cold congealed sausage rolls and lay down on the floor to sleep without saying a word. I pushed him with my foot in the side. He grunted but kept his eyes shut. I kicked harder, this time he opened his eyes. "What happened in Portrush?" I asked.

"Nothing ever happens in Portrush," Knot said and went back to sleep.

# 10

## KILLYBAY TO PEEL

There always seemed to be a big difference between the
departure and the return of the Lady Jane.

On the outward passage the skipper - resplendent in
blue blazer with his gold-braided cap perched jauntily over
one eye - would issue crisp orders to his tidily dressed crew
as they moved speedily around the immaculate vessel.

"Bring the fenders inboard."

"Secure that rope forrard."

"I think a small tot of rum might be in order, Mr Mate."

Each order would be obeyed immediately with a
cheery, "Aye Aye sir."

Compare this with the return journey: Blazer discarded
on the galley floor. Cap lying forlornly in the head.
Skipper roaring through the wheelhouse door, one eye
closed and the other staring madly. "Get that bloody boat-
hook ready; we're going to miss the flaming mooring."

The crew - dishevelled, dirty, blood and oil-stained -
move dispiritedly round the debris, kicking empty bottles
overboard and muttering: "Drunken old bum. Let him
come up here and do it himself if he's so smart."

"I didn't want to come in this rust-bucket anyway."

"Never again."

Not this time however: this time everything went
wrong from the start.

Five o'clock on a May evening is not a good time to
start a voyage of at least three hours, but all SJ would
say was, "Plenty of time. We've got all night to get there."

Finally we were ready to cast off. Then SJ decided that
supplies were a bit low, so Knot was sent to scout for the

necessary liquid provisions. Knot was not a good choice. It took the remainder of the crew to prise him away from the bar of the local hostelry.

It was already beginning to get dark when we crossed the bar, the sun sinking dead astern as we headed blindly for a port that none of us had ever seen before. SJ was on the wheel for the interesting bit - down the lough and into the open sea - but he soon got thirsty and retired to the back of the wheelhouse with Knot, to keep Europe's rum lake from overflowing. This left the controls in the hands of Sammy, Eagle Eye and myself.

Control but not command; SJ left us in no doubt who was in charge, shouting up the wheelhouse every few minutes:

"Check the radar."

"What does the left temperature gauge say?"

"We're heading for that big island over there to your right. No, to the right! Are you blind or stupid? Or both?"

The Isle of Man sits at an angle in the Irish sea with the southern end sticking out towards Ireland. Consequently when one is approaching from the west - as we were - the bottom half of the island is seen much sooner than the top. Also, as the western coastal region is lightly inhabited and there are virtually no lights to be seen, it is difficult to judge at night exactly where one is by sight alone. All I could do was to accept the readings of the machines and try to ignore SJ's advice.

Soon shouting became boring for SJ so he and Knot came staggering up the wheelhouse to give us the benefit of their expertise. SJ decided that we were off course and Knot, knowing where his next drink was coming from, agreed.

"Where is it we're heading anyway?" Knot asked slyly, "Scotland?"

Foolishly I allowed myself to be goaded by this slur on my navigational skills and an argument began. One should never argue with drunks - unless one is drunk oneself of course - then the ridiculous sounds reasonable. It puts all the participants on an even, or uneven, footing so to speak.

Both Knot and SJ liked the crack about Scotland so, even when they went back to the booze, they kept up a running commentary from behind:

"Is that the Mull of Galloway lighthouse flashing over there?"

"Hoots mon.  I think we're lost."

"Mind you don't run into the Stranraer ferry now."

"Don't listen to them," said Sammy, "they'll be lucky if they see Peel tonight the amount they're knocking back."

"Aye, damned lucky," said SJ from behind, "We're headed in the wrong direction."

There was much studying of charts and reading of almanacs as we approached Peel.  It was pitch dark and the light on the end of the harbour wall was barely visible against the lights  from the town.  All went well, however, and we were soon tied up alongside a huge sausage fixed to the harbour wall.  Actually it was a fender which rose and fell with the tide to allow fuel tenders to pump oil to the Isle of Man power station which is located in Peel.

There is not a big sign in most harbours saying welcome to 'Wherever', and this was no exception.  The argument was not over yet.

"You say this is Peel." said SJ "Well prove it.  I bet you haven't a clue where we really are.  Here Knot, shin up a ladder and find out where they've brought us."

Knot was in no condition to shin up anything, but he dutifully stuck his head out through the door and bellowed at a passing seaman.  "Here mate!  What do you call this place?"

"Well?"  SJ demanded as Knot came back in.

"I dunno.  He must have been pissed.  I couldn't make out a word he said."  (The man was off a Russian fishing boat in the harbour.)

Sammy, Eagle Eye and I decided to take a stroll.  We were beginning to get a little worried ourselves about our location and, secretly, wanted to check it out.  Our position said we were in Peel, but the constant niggling by SJ and Knot was starting to sow seeds of doubt.

"Where do you think we are?"  Sammy asked me as soon as we were out of earshot of the Lady Jane.

"I know where we are," I replied forcefully. "We're in Peel, Isle of Man."

"But how do we know for sure?" asked Eagle Eye. "We might be in Scotland. Anywhere."

How can anyone tell where they are if they land in a strange town at night? It may sound strange, but there are very few ways of discovering, short of asking and looking like a complete pillock. We wandered along look-ing at the advertising boards - fags and booze, same as anywhere. Taxi signs - name and telephone number.

A courting couple passed us murmuring to each other. Sammy sidled over towards them, head on one side.

"Eff off!" said the boy, and the couple departed hurriedly, glancing back towards us every now and then.

"I only wanted to hear their accents," Sammy said.

"Tell that to the judge," Eagle Eye replied. "Here come the cops."

The police car slowed but did not stop.  We sauntered on towards the lights of the town.

Another couple came towards us.  They were arguing. "Indeed to bejasus,"  was all we could make out as they passed.

"Dublin?" asked Eagle Eye.

Sammy and Eagle Eye were becoming a little bit hysterical at this stage, each making a suggestion more foolish than the last.

"We could say we were shipwrecked,"  said Sammy. Then he went on to embellish his plan with ideas for us to jump in the sea - to add credence to his story.

"Dial 999,"  said Eagle Eye.  "If they answer we will at least know we are in the United Kingdom."

"We might need Francs for the phone,"  I said sarcastically.

"Is that a Manx cat?"  Eagle Eye  asked suddenly, pointing to a dark shadow which darted across the road in front of us.  He galloped off after the beast with Sammy and I in hot pursuit.  Down the road, round a corner we ran until the cat escaped into a back-yard.  We collapsed on top of the sea wall, panting.

"Why did you think it was a Manx cat?"  Sammy asked. "Hadn't it got a tail?"

"Naw,"  Eagle Eye replied,  "It only had three legs."And, laughing hysterically, he tumbled over the wall.

# 11

## DOUGLAS AT LAST

Douglas had become our holy Grail, our Mecca, eagerly sought but, seemingly, unattainable. For this attempt nothing had been left to chance: The engines and gearboxes had been given a full service. All moving parts were inspected, cleaned and greased. The pumps were checked. Diesel and water tanks were topped up. The crew were hand picked - or rather they picked themselves: we just took anyone who was foolish enough to come along.

Old Bob had been forgiven for past failings and was signed on as cook. He together with Sammy, Eagle Eye, SJ and myself made up the crew.

"Ramsey Coastguard. Ramsey Coastguard. This is Lady Jane. Lady Jane. Over."

I reported to the coastguard, giving our position, E.T.A. and the number of souls on board. Everything by the book. Even the weather was on our side, blue skies, a calm sea, what little breeze there was helping us on towards our goal.

"Do you think there really is such a place as Douglas?" asked Eagle Eye as he, Sammy and I lay stretched out on the deck enjoying the sun. "Or is it like Shangri-La."

"Oh aye," said Sammy. "There definitely is for I have been there."

"And were there lots of wee men with bald heads and wearing orange robes running about?"

"Yes. How did you know that? I thought you said you had never been to Douglas?"

"Just a guess," said Eagle Eye, lying back and closing

his eyes. "Just a guess."

On across the Irish Sea we cruised, through Calf Sound, across Carrickey Bay, round Dreswick Point. A straight run of half an hour and we would be there.

"What are we going to do when we get in?" I asked.

This seemed to puzzle the others; the getting there had been our aim for so long now that the being there was something we had never really considered.

"Let's concentrate on getting there first," said Sammy. "Then we can decide what to do."

Douglas harbour is a busy working port. As we approached a huge passenger ferry backed out towards us. SJ hurriedly cut the engines and we sat there studying the traffic. I called the harbourmaster on channel 12 and was told to wait. The ferry departed and the harbourmaster gave us permission to enter the harbour, directing us to a visitor's pontoon at the end of the Battery Pier. With me pointing, Eagle Eye and Sammy on the sharp end and SJ on the wheel we crept into Douglas harbour.

"What? Over there?" said SJ contemptuously as I pointed to the mooring buoy. "That's no good. We'll have to use the dinghy every time we want to go ashore. What's that over there?" He pointed to an inviting empty wall at the end of a pier. I consulted the chart. "King Edward the Eighth Pier." I read. "And that's the harbourmaster perched on the end of it."

"That'll do," said SJ, spinning the wheel.

Eagle Eye and Sammy, unaware that we were tying up to a wall hurriedly dropped the boat-hook and scrambled about looking for fenders. Sammy managed to protect the side of the Lady Jane just in time and then he hopped off, on to the steps, to tie us up.

A head appeared over the edge of the dark steep wall. It said something to Sammy. He shrugged his shoulders, shook his head and pointed down at us. I quickly found that I was needed in the galley and nipped back to skulk behind the fridge. After two seasons of sailing with SJ I was becoming an expert at hiding.

Sammy stuck his head round the door. "He wants to

see you," he told SJ.

"Well tell him to come on board then," SJ instructed.

Eagle Eye had made himself scarce as well; he was round the blind side of the wheelhouse earnestly examining the state of the deck paint.

The official came on board.

"Sorry I couldn't come up to explain," said SJ "But I have this bad leg. Can hardly walk sometimes."

Slightly mollified the man came on board and sat down. There is a myth that most seafaring men are overly fond of the bottle. A myth that none I have ever met seems eager to dispel. This one was no exception. With a glass of Scotch in his hand he and SJ were soon discussing the relative merits of steel, G.R.P. or wood in boat building while the rest of us crept slowly out to join them.

"You planning to stay here in Douglas overnight?" the official asked.

"If that's alright with you," SJ replied, pouring another whisky.

"Certainly. Of course. I will just have to leave a note in the office as I will be going off duty in a few minutes."

Sammy, Eagle Eye and I set off to explore the town leaving SJ, Bob and the man to it. We never discovered what his title or even his name was. Along the pier and out into the bright lights of Douglas we went. Well actually they were not that bright as it was still broad daylight.

Like most eagerly awaited events our visit to Douglas was a disappointment. "Just like Blackpool," observed Eagle Eye. We wandered along the promenade, looking at the candy-floss machines, the cafes, the gaming machines; just like any other British seaside holiday town.

The food was similar too. After a revolting meal of greasy fish and chips, we headed back towards the boat. A short trip on one of the horse drawn trams took us to the pier and ended our short excursion to Douglas town.

Back on board all was quiet. SJ was sitting in the helmsman's seat, just where we had left him, looking

perfectly normal except that one eye was open more than the other - a sign that he was having trouble focusing. The other pair were lying unconscious on the seats. Bob slumped forward onto his knees, while the harbour official lay flat on his back snoring gently, a glass still grasped in his hand.

"Excuse me," came a timid voice from above.

"He's been shouting for about fifteen minutes," said SJ "See what he wants."

I looked up. A young man was hanging over the rail at the top of the steps.

"Yes," I said.

"I have been told to ask what you're doing here," the young man said.

"We have permission," I replied.

"Oh," he said rather tamely, and disappeared.

Another head appeared. An older man with salt and

He said,... we have permission....
...and will you give him a big kiss!"....

pepper hair peeping out from under his gold-braided hat shouted down. "You there. Who do you say gave you permission to tie up here?"

"He did," I said, pointing into the Lady Jane.

The man advanced down the steps. "Who did?" he asked again.

I indicated the recumbent figure on the seat inside.

"Good Lord. What have you done to him," said the man, stepping back so hurriedly that he almost fell into the harbour.

Having been reassured that we had not murdered his colleague, the official came on board.

"Fancy a drink?" asked SJ hoisting a bottle aloft.

The man glanced at his colleague - I think he probably still considered foul play was involved. "Er - no thanks."

The official helped us to carry the body up the steps and into the berthing master's office. We left him to phone for a taxi and headed back to the Lady Jane.

"Do you think we should move on to a visitor's mooring for the night?" asked Sammy.

"Naw. Bugger it," said SJ, "I'm going to turn in."

The following morning we were getting ready to cast off when a head peeped over the wall; it was SJ's drinking partner from the night before. "Heading off?" he enquired in a strained voice .

"We thought we would take a bit of a cruise," I said. "Maybe spend tonight in Port St Mary."

"Lucky Port St Mary," he said enigmatically, and disappeared from view.

# 12

## DOUGLAS TO RAMSEY

The departure from Douglas was quite uneventful. True one is supposed to contact the harbourmaster and ask permission to leave, but, when this was suggested to SJ he just said: "We were tied up to his steps all night. If he can't see us leaving he should try a different line of work."

As we rounded the Victoria pier SJ put the wheel to port. I moved across to stand beside him. "Aren't you supposed to turn right?" I asked.

"I thought we would have a look at the other end of the island for a change," he said. "I'm getting fed up with the scenery down there."

Handy; I had not even glanced at the chart for the north of the island.

"Well hold her out a bit then," I told him. "Give me a chance to study the coastline."

"On a day like this?" said SJ. "A baby could drive a boat in this sort of weather."

He had a point, it was another glorious day. The sea was so calm that the sudden boiling of the surface, caused by feeding mackerel, was almost obscene. Small boats were dotted about, a puff of smoke showing as the engines were started up to follow the shoals of fish.

"Fancy a lunch of mackerel?" asked SJ spinning the wheel to take us out to where the terns were diving into the green water.

Sammy and Eagle Eye got out the rods and with SJ, Bob and I watching, cast out. Within a few minutes each had caught a couple of fish, and the bug really caught hold of all of us. We squabbled over the rods like schoolboys, letting innumerable fish escape in the process. By the time we had settled whose turn it was the shoal had moved on, so we joined the dozen or so other boats cruising round in circles.

An hour passed, the fishing was good and we had about two dozen mackerel in a basket on top of the galley roof.

"Nip below and get me a sweater," SJ told Sammy. It was getting rather chilly. The early morning heat had gone and there was a dampness in the air.

Sammy came back with a sweater for SJ. "All the other boats have gone," he observed on his return. We looked around. Save for a huge oil-tanker on the horizon we were alone. Looking towards the shore a single small boat was just entering a huge bank of fog which rolled down off the mountains and was reaching out to engulf us.

Douglas is particularly subject to these sudden radiation mists. Known locally as Manin mists they are sent by the sea-god Manamanin to protect the island from invaders. He was doing a good job that morning; no sensible invader would have dared attempt a landing.

"Will it get our length, do you think?" asked Sammy.

No sooner asked than answered. The mist rolled out to reach, then cover the Lady Jane. Hastily we turned on the radar. Even though, five minutes before, we had been able to see clearly around us and we were off the main shipping routes, there is a fear, a dread, about being blind at sea.

"Start the engines." said SJ "We'll stand off a bit. We should be able to outrun it."

The engines were started and we motored off. This made things even more frightening as we were now unable to hear what was going on outside. A foghorn sounded. The radar showed a huge blip about three miles off and not heading towards us, but it sounded so close that we all held our breath. Eagle Eye was sent out on deck with the hand-held foghorn. He popped his head back in almost immediately. "Aren't I supposed to give some sort of a special signal?" he asked.

"Just let them know where we bloody well are," yelled SJ.

I hunted through the almanac and found the signals. Eagle Eye was signalling madly. One long, two short - meaning a vessel not under command. Perhaps he had subconsciously remembered it from somewhere and his true feelings for the captain of the Lady Jane were showing through.

Scanning the chart I asked SJ: "How far offshore do you think we are?"

"About a mile," he replied, standing up to peer through the window.

"About half a mile I'd guess," said Sammy. "What do you think Bob?"

Bob did not get a chance to reply. "Nobody piggin' asked you," snapped SJ. "Now get outside and keep your eyes open."

"What now?" SJ asked me.

"Stand off a bit more," I suggested. "Then, when we're sure we're clearing Clay Head, turn north and take it very easy until the fog lifts."

It was a good plan and it probably would have worked, had Eagle Eye not seen the lobster pot marker too late. Just as he yelled a warning the starboard engine laboured, then died. This meant two things: One, we were probably nearer the shore than we thought we were. And two, we had very restricted manoeuvrability with only one engine.

"We'll have to cut it off," said SJ.

"Who do you mean when you say we?" asked Sammy, paling.

"Nothing to it," said SJ handing Sammy a pair of goggles and a knife.

"Well you do it then," said Sammy, shoving them back.

Sammy was persuaded and we all trekked to the stern to help him - mainly with advice. A rope round his middle, and wearing a life jacket, Sammy lowered himself over the edge and into the water. He blew hard, took a deep breath and pushed himself under the water. Back up he popped almost immediately. "What's the matter?" SJ shouted down at him.

Sammy tried again, but once more the life jacket forced him to the surface. He climbed back on board. "Can't be done," Sammy said, handing the knife back to SJ.

"Here Robert," SJ handed me the knife. "Show this wee girl how to do it."

Sammy stripped off the life jacket, grabbed the knife from me and jumped overboard. "Wee girl," we heard him muttering, then a lot of splashing, then silence. We waited. Nothing.

"Pull that bloody rope up," SJ said.

We pulled; it came up free - no Sammy. SJ was looking quite panicky when Sammy surfaced, waving a buoy attached to a piece of rope. "Easy." he chattered through blue lips. We pulled him back on board, wrapped him in a blanket, and re-started the engines. "Straight out?" SJ asked me. I nodded. We crept forward, me on the radar, SJ on the wheel and Eagle Eye back on the bows. Bob was feeding Sammy with hot soup, trying to save him from hypothermia.

When we judged that we were about a mile offshore I asked SJ to turn due north. We crept up the coast, trying to mirror our course with the radar image. A large blip showed on the screen, heading straight for us. We headed out to sea, the other vessel swung out too, our courses converging. 'Coincidence' I thought, and asked SJ to bring the Lady Jane round again. Once more the blip on the screen altered course to approach us head on.

"What's wrong?" Sammy asked, abandoning his soup and coming up to the wheelhouse to join me.

"We have a kamikaze captain, trying to run us down."

She was getting close, too close; Eagle Eye ran down the deck and stuck his head in the door. "I can hear something big," he said.

"Well get up forward and blow that thing," SJ told him, sweat starting to show on his brow.

"We'll wait until we see her, then I can use full power to get out of her way," SJ said.

We held our breath. Eagle Eye gave one last despairing note on the foghorn and dodged back to cower beside the wheelhouse. The bows of the other ship appeared, cutting a white swathe through the water. SJ swung the wheel and shoved the throttles fully forward. We scooted out from under the deadly shadow of the ship and escaped to rock violently in its wake. Not a soul was seen on the other vessel. Huge containers were piled high on the well, lights showed clearly on the bridge, but there seemed to be no lookouts - no one on board at all.

We decided to go inshore a bit and anchor until the fog lifted.

"The Lady Jane is so small - compared to them - that the other ship probably thought we were just a piece of wreckage," said Eagle Eye.

"Well they wouldn't be far wrong," said Sammy.

# 13

## ESCORT DUTY

"Excuse me." Sammy and I looked at each other in surprise. We were being addressed by a yacht owner - the type of person who normally regarded us as if we were something he had just wiped off the soles of his shoes.

We had called into Port Erin that Sunday afternoon, on our way back from Douglas, to get a meal before the last leg of our journey back to Killybay. SJ and Old Bob had stayed on board while Sammy and I stretched our legs. The man who had accosted us was a tall thin individual, dressed in 'proper' yachting clothes - unlike the rags which we felt it appropriate to wear on any lengthy journey on the Lady Jane."Are you going back home soon?" the man continued.

Still surprised Sammy and I made no reply so the yachtsman continued. "There are three of us who need to get home today - my name is Chubb by the way - and, with this wind blowing, we are going to have to go across under power. When we saw you coming in we thought you might accompany us, as an escort, if you didn't mind."

There was a force seven blowing directly onshore, and Mr Chubb - or Captain Chubb as we came to call him - was hanging grimly on to his peaked cap. "We'll have to ask the skipper." I told him, and Sammy and I headed back to the Lady Jane.

"No bloody way!" said SJ forcefully when we relayed the request. "I'm not going to hang about in this weather waiting for those ponces."

"Er-hem." There was a noise from behind. Captain Chubb had followed us back and was standing on the breakwater looking in through the open wheelhouse door.

"SJ?" he asked.

"Who wants to know?" SJ growled back.

"I believe you know one of our number - Dr Johnston."

"Not the Dr Johnston?" I said brightly. All four of them stared blankly at me so I shut up.

"Charlie?" said SJ, and Captain Chubb nodded. "Oh I know Charlie," SJ continued. "Many a great night we had in the Queen's Arms." Again a quip sprang to my lips but, wisely, I kept it to myself.

The details were worked out: the three yachts would put to sea almost immediately, the tide being on the turn. We would follow as soon as they passed the breakwater and try to keep station with them. A radio channel was selected for communication, with me as the controller.

Port Erin harbour is completely ringed by high cliffs making radio communication with the outside world almost impossible, so it was not until we were at sea that I was able to contact the coastguard and tell them of our crossing.

"Say again," came back the reply when I contacted Ramsey.

I repeated the names of the four vessels, the number of souls on board, our E.T.A. and the fact that we were doing escort.

"Are you the cruiser that was in Port Erin a couple of months ago? The white one?" asked the coastguard.

"Yes," I replied.

As the coastguard keyed his mike I could just make out a voice behind him saying: "Gawd help them." But the man on the radio just wished us a safe crossing and asked me to let him know how we were getting on.

The seas were fairly rough. White water broke over the bows every few minutes, the occasional larger wave washing the full length of the Lady Jane. She would plough bravely on, giving a little shake to rid herself of the water to prepare for the next onslaught. We were forced to travel at the speed of the slowest boat, a twenty-five foot ketch with a very small auxiliary engine. To break the monotony SJ would describe a huge circle round the three yachts, like a sheepdog round its flock, but every time we came broadside to the waves it became very uncomfortable so he was persuaded to give it up.

We had been at sea for about two hours when the radio burst into life. It was Charlie Johnston. His engine was overheating and he did not think he could coax it along much further.

The coastguard broke in almost immediately asking if we required any assistance?

"Tell him to piss off," said SJ

I relayed the message that we were okay for the moment and we prepared to go to the rescue. Sammy and I went on deck. It was almost impossible to stand on the wildly bucking foredeck so we worked our way round behind the wheelhouse. We waited in its shelter until SJ brought the Lady Jane right round behind the stricken yacht and then alongside. I had tied a rope to the handrail on the cabin roof, and with this round my waist I held grimly on to the back of Sammy's lifejacket. As the two boats came level Sammy tossed a line across and this was grabbed by Charlie who pulled it, and the heavier line attached to it, across.

Sammy and I made our way back, fixed the tow-rope to the stern cleats and went to report to SJ. Charlie called on the radio to say that his end of the line was fixed so off we went. Even with the added weight of our tow we soon caught up with the other two yachts and our convoy was back together again.

A small aircraft appeared swooping down from the cloudy sky to almost wave height. It droned over, turned and came back for another look. As it approached, head-on, we ducked involuntarily as it roared past. The pilot could clearly be seen watching us through his windscreen. The coastguard came back on the radio. "I hear you have successfully taken the yacht in tow," he said.

"How does he know that?" Sammy asked.

"That bugger in the plane is reporting to him. That's how," said SJ

Five long slow hours passed before we approached the coast. Captain Chubb came on the radio again. His boat could only make five knots and the tide, streaming out of the lough, was at least six. He thanked us and said they would anchor and wait for the tide to turn before proceeding. We motored on, SJ holding the Lady Jane close to the shore to avoid the worst effects of the tide.

As we came in to the lough proper it was much calmer so SJ decided that Sammy should fix Charlie's engine. He bought the Lady Jane up to speed then threw the engines into reverse. As we slowed Charlie's boat came alongside and, with me feverishly gathering up the tow rope before it caught in the props, Sammy stepped over on to the yacht. "It'll be the raw water intake," SJ yelled at Sammy as the yacht dropped astern again.

By the time we reached Killybay Charlie was back

67

under his own steam.  He dropped the tow, I pulled it on board and, while we moored, Charlie carried on to his mooring at the yacht club taking Sammy with him.

While we waited for Sammy, SJ, Bob and I tidied up. Bob and I packed lockers and brushed the floor while SJ tried to make sure that all the bottles on board were empty.  I let the dinghy down off the stern davits, brought it round and put our bags into it - all ready for the off. Sammy, Charlie and Mrs Johnston arrived, Charlie clutching a bottle of scotch which he presented to SJ. Ceremoniously SJ unscrewed the top from the bottle and threw it overboard.  "We won't be needing that again," he announced.

After about an hour the bottle was almost empty and we were looking forward to getting home.  The other two boats arrived however and both their skippers decided to show their appreciation in the same way as Charlie had. Armed with two new bottles SJ held court on the Lady Jane.

Mrs Johnston was anxious to get home, so I volunteered to take her ashore and give her a lift in SJ's car.  The party was in full swing as we left, Sammy attempting to jump ship as well but prevented by SJ saying: "Sit there and behave yourself.  We'll only be a minute."

"At least some good has come of it," I told my wife over a late supper.  "We should be back in the good books of the local sailing fraternity.  No more cold shoulders in the bar."  I was reckoning without SJ  Sammy told me the following day that he had thrown all of his guests off the Lady Jane shortly after I had left.  "You ought to have heard what he called Captain Chubb, too."  SJ took much longer to get home that his unfortunate guests, though.  He had forgotten that I had taken the Lady Jane's dinghy so he and Sammy spent the night aboard, not getting ashore until they managed to beg a lift from a passing fisherman.

# 14

## PRACTICE MAKES PERFECT

We were just out for the day. SJ, Sammy, Eagle Eye and SJ's daughter, Carrie, collected me and we drove down to Killybay. For once we had judged the tide just right and we swept down the lough at a good speed with very little effort from the engines.

As we approached the narrows the ferry was putting out from the northern shore. "Watch out," said Sammy, pointing.

"Do you think I'm blind," SJ snapped back.

Because of the strength of the tide the ferry is forced to go up or down the lough, fighting the current, until the skipper decides he has reached the right position. Then the boat is turned, and with the tide assisting, swoops easily to the other side - arriving opposite where it started from after a journey of perhaps twice the distance. Normal rules of the road do not apply, and the ferry is not prepared to give up any of its hard-earned progress - especially to pleasure boaters.

We got closer. Sammy cleared his throat. SJ kept on course. I decided to intervene: "Don't you think she's getting a bit close?"

"He'll be turning any second now," said SJ. Then, as the ferry still approached: "Any second."

"For God's sake!" Sammy cried reaching for the wheel. Just with that the ferry turned for her berth on the far side. We slipped behind her, bouncing over the wake. A window high on the ferry opened and a head and shoulders appeared through it, gesticulating wildly and shouting. The oaths of the captain were still ringing in our ears when

SJ said smugly: "Told you."

On down the lough we went. I pointed out any other vessels and SJ carefully, and uncharacteristically, avoided them. The bar was perfectly calm and we sailed safely and easily into the open sea.

On round the coast. We decided to put into Ardmore harbour for lunch, not having any provisions on board. As we approached the entrance to the harbour a fishing boat came ploughing out, tight against the wall, and not visible until she was almost on top of us.

"Stupid git!" SJ roared, spinning the wheel to avoid the other boat and almost putting us onto the rocks on the opposite side of the entrance.

The Lady Jane is not a manoeuvrable boat; when SJ stuck an extra nine feet into the middle of her he put in bigger engines but left the rudders the way they were. Despite much advice to the contrary he refused to change them, insisting that the Lady Jane was perfect. With a bit of speed on she was usually fine, and when it came to berthing we would always try to slide straight in, the crew getting a line ashore as quickly as possible to pull in whichever end did not make it alongside. SJ's nervousness after our near miss with the ferry meant we finished up in the middle of Ardmore harbour and, due to a lack of room to manoeuvre, we were forced to approach the wall head on.

Sammy and I had the fenders ready: I was at the bows so was able to stand and wait but Sammy, at the stern, had to try and decide which side SJ was going to put to the wall. He danced back and forth nervously before giving up, tying a fender to each side and joining me at the front. SJ was trying to decide between speed and turning ability. With no speed the Lady Jane just went straight on. Too much speed and, when she did hit, she would do so that much harder. Hundreds of enthralled spectators lined the wall, as far as I know they did not turn up to see us dock - more to do with the fishing - but they took the opportunity of some free entertainment and craned their necks to see the fun.

SJ sweated and swore, but still the Lady Jane would

not turn. He put one engine full ahead and the other full astern, at last something was beginning to happen - too late, we were going to hit the wall. I dropped a fender between the bows and the wall. It took the strain, bulged out on either side of the bows, then bounced us back. Sammy tossed a rope on to the wall. Small boys fought over it until one, slightly bigger than the rest and wearing a red tee-shirt, grabbed it and held it aloft. "What do you want me to do with this?" he asked Sammy, peering down over the wall nervously.

"Tie it on to something," Sammy shouted up, adding, "Something big."

The rope fixed, Sammy pulled experimentally on it; It held. There was only one way we could go now as there was a trawler tied to the wall about twenty feet to our right. SJ nudged the starboard engine into gear. The Lady Jane moved slowly forward, then sat butting her head against the wall - churning up mud from the bottom. A slight touch astern with the port engine got us going. Ever so slowly the stern came round heading for the wall, the rope at the bows rubbing up the wall and groaning at the strain as it held us in. The red-shirted boy strutted self-importantly back to take the stern rope, elbowing mere spectators out of his way. Sammy coiled the rope and prepared to throw it to the boy. SJ decided on a final flourish for the crowd, which was beginning to lose interest and drift away: he gave the starboard engine a quick rev to push the stern round. The extra strain was too much for the boy's knot and with a loud twang it let go. Like a greyhound released from the slips the Lady Jane shot down the wall. Sammy grabbed the rail and just managed to stop himself being flung over the stern. I fell back-wards on top of the cabin roof and was just staggering to my feet when we struck the trawler. Luckily it was a steel boat and suffered very little harm. The same could not be said of the Lady Jane. The pulpit rails struck first, crumpling up to allow the peak right in against the curved bows of the trawler. As the metal tore the anchor roller popped out of its mountings and

".....what a helpful child!"

shot past my ear. Engines full astern we pulled back, pieces of metal falling into the harbour. Desperate to get away SJ swung the Lady Jane forward and out, the stern fender bounced us off the trawler and we were back in the open harbour. A white-faced figure emerged from the hold of the trawler. "Alright Frank?" shouted Sammy across the widening gap. Frank waved weakly back and gazed over the stern shaking his head sadly from side to side.

The nearest port to Ardmore is Coolkee, about five miles away, so it was there we headed next. There were no other boats against the wall and, as we slid inch-perfect into our chosen spot, not one person to admire our skill. SJ held the Lady Jane just touching the wall, with the engines while we tied her up.

"Couldn't you have done that in Ardmore?" Sammy asked.

"Do you think you could have done any better?" SJ retorted.

While Carrie went into the village to buy some food Sammy proceeded to show SJ how it should be done. The ropes were let go and we cruised round the harbour. Sammy wanted to approach the wall as SJ had just done, but that was too easy. A position similar to that which we had experienced in Ardmore was adopted and SJ said: "Now bring her in, smartass."

Sammy revved, sweated and swore - sounding more like his father every minute - but still the Lady Jane would not respond as he wanted. When the bows were in the stern was out, and vice-versa. "Bundle of scrap!" Sammy said at last and abandoned the controls. My turn; I sneaked into a position where I was able to approach the wall at a slight angle, flipping the starboard engine control into reverse every few seconds to try and bring the Lady Jane parallel with the wall as we approached. It worked beautifully, we glided majestically in to lie perfectly against the wall just as we grounded on the sloping pebble beach. SJ elbowed me out of the way, "You would have been okay if the wall had been a hundred foot longer," he observed as he reversed us back to tie up.

Carrie arrived back with the provisions so the engines were cut and we settled down to have some lunch. A picnic was being enjoyed on the foredeck when an old man came riding slowly down the quay on a bicycle. Carefully he propped his bike against a stone bollard and wandered over to inspect the Lady Jane.

"Accident?" he said at last, nodding towards the damaged bows.

"No thanks," said SJ "We've just had one."

# 15

## PORT ERIN AGAIN

Douglas here we come.  We had a few days off and were going to spend them in the capital of the Isle of Man.

The weather was perfect - blue skies, calm sea - and the Lady Jane was behaving perfectly.  "Nothing can stop us this time." said Sammy.  He, together with Eagle Eye, SJ and myself made up the crew.

Two and a half hours out from Killybay and already the passage through Calf Sound was opening up to us. We had just passed between Kitterland and Thousla when the noise started.  The same engine as always - the port - was up to its old tricks.  A high pitched whine was coming from the back of the engine accompanied by the smell of burning rubber.

Calf sound is not a good place to stop and do running repairs.  Even on a calm day like this there was a notice-able swell and, as SJ reduced the revs, we could feel the boat being turned towards the rocks of Kitterland.  These two islands are named after a notorious Viking raider, Kitter, after he had wrecked his ship on them with the loss of all the crew.

There was nothing else for it but to turn back to Port Erin.  Once clear of Calf sound the floorboards were ripped up - we were becoming quite expert at this by now - so that we could assess the damage.  The smell was coming from the coupling between the engine and the gearbox.  Smoke was rising off the metal enclosure hold-ing the rubber plugs in place.

And so to Port Erin, slowly.  Tied up to the breakwater we were able to remove the cover from the joint and do a

proper diagnosis. The welding on the round metal cover had broken, allowing it to drop against the revolving rubber constant velocity joints. What we needed was a new cover, but where to get one was the question.

Help was at hand. A replica of Captain Bird's Eye stuck his head round the door. "Permission to come on board?" Once this had been granted he came in with an alacrity which belied his hundred odd years (or so it appeared at first glance.) An old salt; probably sailed round the horn in a tea clipper. (Actually he had been an insurance salesman in Chorley and was sixty four.) Charlie was sailing round the British Isles in a Cornish Crabber and was more nautical than Nelson. He would never dream of tying a rope: "Bend that sheet," he would say, and he was forever belaying as well. "Belay this; Belay that."

"I think I'll go below and belay the table for lunch," said Eagle Eye.

Charlie informed us that there was a boatyard in Ramsey where we should be able to get the part. "I'll take you up there on Monday morning if you like," he offered.

It was a Saturday and, given our past experience of Port Erin, we wanted to get out of it as quickly as possible. Local people greeted us with phrases like: "What's wrong now then?" and "Not berthing on the beach this time?"

Sammy and I volunteered to see if we could find something locally to make the repairs. Armed with the cover we set out on the long familiar walk into the centre of Port Erin. A local boatman informed us that the only workshop thereabouts was in Port St Mary and that it would undoubtedly be closed. "Try them on Monday," he advised.

On into the town. "A garage," Sammy suggested, "we would probably find a welder in a garage. If we beat this thing into shape, we could re-weld the seam, and we will be in Douglas tonight."

Oh if only things were that simple.

There was a garage. It had a welder. The snag was that the garage owner was off for the day and the two young girls who had been left in charge were not authorised to allow anyone to use the equipment.

"Could we have a look?" Sammy asked. "If the equipment suits then we could arrange to come back when the boss is here."Reluctantly one of the girls produced a set of keys and let us into the cool, dark, oil-smelling interior. Sammy was at home right away. "Oh look. He's got a crypton tuner. And look over there - there's an old lathe." He turned to the younger, and better-looking, of the two girls. "I've got one the same as that, only bigger." She seemed suitably impressed.

The bell went. The older girl looked hard at her companion and, getting no response said, "I'll get that. Don't touch anything until I come back."

It seemed that Sammy and the younger girl, Samantha, shared an interest in motorbikes. She volunteered to show him a seven fifty which her father kept out the back. "Find a hammer and beat that into shape," Sammy

said to me and, tossing the cover over, he followed Samantha through a door at the back of the garage.

I was merrily beating away at the cover when the older girl came back from serving petrol. "I thought I said not to touch anything," she said, then, "Here, where's me sister?" I gestured to the door at the back. "She's only sixteen," said the girl as she hurried out through the door. Sixteen seemed quite old enough to be showing off motorbikes, so I didn't panic, but carried on panel-beating instead. Sammy and the two girls came back in. Like any hot-blooded young man Sammy was carried away by his latest discovery. "You ought to see her," he enthused, "Siamese pipes, racing fairing, the lot." Samantha did not seem to have retained her interest in bikes and stood around looking huffy. Her older sister was a little more friendly however and, when I told her the cover was finished - apart from a small tack - she agreed to let me use the electric welder for a minute.

Back we headed for the boat, repaired cover in hand. "Half an hour should stick this thing on," said Sammy, "Then it's off to the bright lights of Douglas." Fat chance.

In our absence SJ had decided to investigate the cause of the failure. Eagle Eye and Charlie were in the bowels of the boat ripping bits off while SJ sat in his chair, issuing orders. A couple of half-empty bottles - or half-full depending on your point of view - sat on the chart table. Charlie's face, that part of it not covered in hair anyway, was bright red and his nautical vocabulary had got worse, if that was possible, since we had left. "I think it's possible that the port engine has been mounted abaft the plimsoll line and a cant of some degree with the prop shaft is causing vibration." (Something like that - I think he meant it wasn't straight.)

SJ looked at Charlie for a moment before replying. "Are you going to be here long?" he asked eventually.

"Aye," Charlie said. "A few days anyway. Why do you ask?"

"Well," SJ replied, "if we need advice from a dickhead I wanted to know where to find one."

Charlie had been sitting on the battery box. "Really!"

he squeaked and stood up quickly. He bashed his head on the cross-member and sat down again even more quickly. "Ohhh," he said. Eagle Eye shoved a glass of whisky into Charlie's hand. He drank, shook his head a few times and said, "Now where were we? Oh yes. Don't you think the shaft is out of alignment?"

SJ insisted that we prove to Charlie that the shaft was perfectly true. Once all the parts had been put back where they should be, a clockguage was produced from SJ's private toolbox and clamped on to the side of the boat. Carefully following SJ's instructions Eagle Eye moved the pointer until it just touched the shaft. With the Lady Jane lashed tightly fore and aft the engine was started and run up. "What's the reading?" SJ roared down from above, as the prop churned up sand and mud from the bottom.

"Zero," Eagle Eye yelled back.

SJ stopped the engine and leant back contentedly. "Fancy another drink friend?" he asked Charlie. The rest of us gave up on the idea of Douglas and wandered up the street to find something to eat.

# 16

## A SUNDAY SAIL

We had decided to make a day of it. Mo was taking his speedboat out and, as there was no slipway in Killybay, we were to meet him and his girlfriend Carrie in Bagnor.

Sammy, SJ and I sailed the Lady Jane round the coast and tied up safely in the harbour. As there was no sign of Mo, Sammy and I decided to take a walk in the marina. To get into the marina one has to pass through a gateway and past a reception area. A young man glanced up as we approached then, as we walked through the gates, he shot off his chair and out of the door to confront us.

"Yes?" the young man said disdainfully, looking us up and down.

"We were just going to have a look around," I said.

"Private," the boy said and started to turn away.

"Well how are we supposed to decide if we want to berth our boat here?" Sammy asked of the departing youth.

"You have a boat?"

"Aye," Sammy said. "That's her there," and he pointed across the harbour to the Lady Jane.

We could see the youth counting the rent that he had almost let slip through his fingers.

"Just let me get you a brochure," he said scuttling back into the office. He presented the literature to Sammy. "Do you want someone to show you round?" he asked.

We declined and wandered round the marina admiring the craft. On our way back out the young man stopped us again. "Would you like to fill in an application form?" he asked.

"No thanks," said Sammy, adding as we left, "Too down-market for us."

Mo and Carrie had arrived by the time we got back, Mo's speedboat had already been launched and was tied to the side of the Lady Jane. After a spot of lunch we set off; Carrie and Mo in the speedboat, the rest of us in the Lady Jane. Once clear of the harbour Mo decided he wanted to waterski and, as he needed a driver, I transferred from the Lady Jane to the speedboat, SJ and Mo keeping the two boats together while I clambered from one to the other.

After a while we tired of skiing and decided we would like some ice-cream. We pulled up alongside the Lady Jane to discuss the relative merits of various makes and where we might buy them. Caffolas' in Donagh was selected and Mo and I elected to go ahead and find a berth for the Lady Jane. Carrie was hauled aboard the Lady Jane and Mo and I set off. Up until this point I had been driving, but Mo took over the controls and decided to show me what his boat could do. We approached Donagh harbour at an incredible speed. As the wall approached I tried to say something to Mo. Something like, "Slow down please". But all that came out were strange garbled grunts from somewhere deep in my chest. I was pinned back in the seat by the speed, and the drumming of the hull as it planed across the tiny wavelets made it impossible to speak. I can only estimate what speed we were doing, about seventy I would say, as we entered the harbour. A speedboat, unlike a displacement craft, slows very quickly so, when Mo knocked the revs off it was like putting on the brakes. "Okay?" Mo asked .

"Yeah. No problem," I stammered nonchalantly, trying to control the trembling in my legs.

We cruised around the harbour looking for a spot to tie up the Lady Jane. Most of Donagh harbour dries at low water so we were trying to find something near the entrance. The Lady Jane came into the harbour. Mo waved SJ across to the berth we had selected while I climbed up the wall to take the ropes. SJ looked at where I was waiting and shouted out through the open door. "Too shallow."

There was a vacant mooring right in the deepest part of the harbour. As SJ was backing out again Mo indicated this mooring to him and shouted that we would bring the ice-cream out to them there. SJ gave the thumbs up and turned in a circle round the harbour. We could see Sammy pick up the boathook and go forward to catch the mooring. First try he got it but, once again, SJ decided there was too little water and decided to leave the harbour altogether. He pushed the throttles forward and we could hear the deepening note of the engines as the Lady Jane gathered speed. Sammy had just got a good grip on the mooring when SJ increased the revs; he said later that he heard the engines increase speed but thought that they had been put into reverse to stop the boat. With a jerk the rope tightened and Sammy was pulled, arm first, right over the safety rail. He described a beautiful dive straight into the harbour. Luckily the mooring was slightly off the course of the Lady Jane so Sammy landed clear of the boat and was saved a keel-hauling and an encounter with the props.

We waited for the Lady Jane to stop and pick Sammy up but she continued on her way. As the noise of the Lady Jane's engines decreased so we could hear the sounds coming from Sammy, as he struggled in the oily, muddy waters of the harbour: "Stupid, blind, deaf, drunken old sod." Then he would cough and splash and start again, his description of his father liberally sprin-kled with swear words.

With Sammy safely in the speedboat we set out after the Lady Jane. SJ was relaxing quite happily in the helms-man's chair as we came alongside. We never said a word, but cruised along beside the Lady Jane waiting for SJ to notice something. Carrie came forward from the galley and stood at the door. She stared at Sammy then, with a puzzled look on her face, said something to SJ He screwed round in his seat, looked down into the speedboat and knocked the throttles to neutral. We sat there looking at one another for some time, the two boats bumping in what little breeze there was that sunny afternoon.

It was SJ who finally broke the silence. "Who told you

to change boats?" he asked Sammy.

That opened the floodgates. Sammy stormed, ranted and raved. He jumped about so much that, afraid of going into the water ourselves, Mo and I calmed him down and helped him aboard the Lady Jane for a change of clothes.

That put an end to our day's outing. We said goodbye to Mo and Carrie, waved them off and headed back for Killybay - SJ and Sammy studiously not talking to one another.

In the narrows of the sea lough, on which Killybay is set, there is a particularly dangerous stretch of water. As the tide sweeps in and out millions of tons of water confined by the narrow inlet, create whirlpools and overfalls which has swept many an unwary seafarer to their doom. As we came up the lough that day there was a small motorboat drifting about in one of the particularly bad sections of the narrows.

"Funny place to be fishing," said SJ as we passed, about a hundred yards away from the boat.

The occupants of the boat were waving at us. Nothing unusual about that - people quite often waved at the Lady Jane, usually with their fists.

"Is there something wrong with them?" said Sammy.

With the glasses I could see that the waves being made in our direction were for help. Three people were in the boat, two men waving madly and a girl huddled in fear on the stern seat.

"I suppose we'd better get them out of there," said SJ, swinging the Lady Jane round.

The boat was caught in the outer edges of the whirlpool, drifting round helplessly and being inexorably drawn towards the centre. As we neared the stricken craft Sammy and I went forward, ropes ready to throw across the decreasing gap.

With the rope firmly fixed to the motorboat SJ backed the Lady Jane out of the maelstrom. Once we were in calmer water I shifted the tow round to the stern cleats and we had time to examine our catch. It seemed they had simply run out of fuel, each of the two men thinking

the other had checked the tank.  We found out where they wanted to be towed to and, having landed them safely, carried on for Killybay.

"Do you know something?" said SJ reaching for the bottle.

"What's that?" I asked.

"Some people just aren't safe to be let out in a boat."

# 17

## LAYING A MOORING.

We had spent most of the summer lying at a visitors mooring so the local council was, understandably, annoyed.

SJ showed me the letter. What it said in effect was: "Get your boat moved". Never one to do something himself, when anyone else was available, SJ told me to ring Walter - a boatman in Killybay - and find out how much it would cost.

"Two hundred pounds," he roared when I came off the phone.

"And you have to provide the mooring," I added.

"No way," SJ said forcefully, "I'll lay it myself first."

I tried my best to talk him out of it; when SJ said 'I' he usually meant 'us', with him giving the orders and the rest of us doing the sweating.

Once having made his mind up there was no holding SJ. My next phone call was to the railway company: "Yes they had wheels available and, yes we could collect them right away." Knot was sent off to collect two, while Sammy was told to get some chain ready.

"Where are you going to get the chain?" I asked, "You'll need a good heavy one for the ground chain."

It seemed that SJ had bought some chain two years before, in anticipation of this day. He could quite happily wait two years but, now that he had decided to lay the mooring himself, he could not even wait until the weekend.

The chain was put into the trailer along with the two railway wagon wheels which Knot had brought home. We stopped at a local agricultural merchants and bought some heavy galvanised shackles. "All systems are go," said SJ as we sped down the road towards Killybay.

SJ's estimation of Walter's price seemed fair as the afternoon wore on. First one of the railway wheels was shackled to the ground chain and dropped off the side of the quay. Next the Lady Jane was brought alongside, the wheel winched up to just above the surface, and we were ready to let go.

"Where are you going to drop it?" asked Sammy. Nobody had really considered this aspect of the job before and, looking around the crowded moorings, it seemed we might have a problem.

"Right there," said SJ pointing straight ahead, "Plenty of room, and it will be handy for the dinghy."

"Surely that has to be kept clear for the quay," I said. "A fairway, I think it's called."

"That's golf," said SJ.

It was as simple as clockwork. We dropped the new mooring and secured our mooring strap to the ground chain. Then, using a fender as a temporary float, we gave the Lady Jane a couple of turns with the engines to make sure we were clearing everything and we were off.

"Three hours," said SJ contemptuously, "and that swine Walter was going to charge us two hundred pounds. Huh!"

"But won't she just float off?" asked Sammy. "If we could carry the wheel out what's to stop her carrying it away?"

Patiently, for once, SJ explained. "She will lie to the mooring. As the tide rises the ground chain will come up a little bit, but not enough to raise the mooring from the bottom. You don't think an oil-tanker has a ten thousand ton weight attached to it's mooring do you?"

An excellent explanation. However when one takes a twenty foot chain, wraps it round a wheel, sinks it in the mud beneath ten feet of water - at low tide - and then adds a thirteen foot tide, the sums go a little bit awry.

Walter phoned the following morning, in some glee, to break the good news. SJ rang us all right away. "She's dragged the mooring," he informed me without so much as a 'good morning': "Get in here right away."

Sammy and I extricated the Lady Jane - our mooring had got tangled with someone else's - and brought her in to the quay where SJ and Knot were waiting.

"More weight," SJ decided. "We'll put the second wheel on."

"Not me," I said. "Not now anyway. I have work to go to."

"And I have that machine to fix in Belfast," said Sammy. "Has to be done this morning."

Back onto the visitor's mooring went the Lady Jane, with an agreement that we would all meet back at the quay that evening.

Sammy had some sense, he didn't turn up. Knot and I manoeuvred the second wheel into position and started up the electric winch. It gave a few whines and stopped. "Never mind," said SJ. "There's a manual handle lying

for fifty quid, I bought the whole engine!

about somewhere below."

With Knot on the handle, me on the rope and SJ sitting watching, we somehow got the wheel hoisted off the bottom.

Walter wandered up the quay and stood watching us sweat, hands in pockets. "Don't give up your day jobs." He advised before moving on.

After another half an hour's heaving and puffing we finally got the wheel clear of the water. We motored slowly out, bows down, to where our fender floated forlornly on the darkening water. Our next problem was to find the shackle which joined the ground chain to the strap. This was below water and, with the winch already in use, try as we might we could not pull enough up to expose it.

"We'll just have to wait for the tide to go out," SJ decided, opening a bottle of rum: "Anyone fancy a shot?"

Two hours later, with the aid of a torch, I could just make out the shackle as it cleared the water. The shackle was too large however to go through the hole in the wheel. "No hurry," said SJ pouring another drink. "There will be plenty of slack at low tide."

Another hour slowly passed. From the dinghy I unscrewed the bolt from the shackle and tied a piece of rope to the ground chain. In almost total darkness I went hand over hand back to the ladder where Knot waited to take the rope. Then back to the bows, the dinghy swinging under my feet and trying its best to throw me into the sea. Knot and SJ's job was to pass the rope through the centre of the wheel and re-connect the strap to the ground chain. The wheel could then be let go, sliding down the ground chain to rest on top of the first wheel on the bottom.

SPLASH! Everything went according to plan. I tumbled SJ and Knot into the dinghy, got us ashore, left their car on the quay and drove them home. "That should hold her now," SJ said as I dropped him off.

A week passed. Walter phoned again - same message. Back to the visitor's mooring - I don't know why the council complained, no one used it but us. This time, however, someone - SJ swore it was Walter - cut the fender off our chain while we were away, allowing it to fall to the bottom.

On the following Sunday afternoon we sent down Mo and a friend of his who was in a sub-aqua club to find the chain. After an age searching in the mud of the bottom they came up to report. "We found your mooring," said Mo, "and the second wheel, but they're not connected in any way."

SJ and Knot each insisted that the other had been responsible for putting the chain through the centre of the wheel - or not putting it through as seemed to be the case.

Back to the visitor's mooring.

Luckily Walter needed some work done on his boat so a trade-off was arranged. The mooring, professionally laid, has kept us safe ever since at a cost, estimated by Sammy, of only one thousand pounds.

# 18

## THE TRAWLER RACE

Every year at a local fishing port there is an end-of-season trawler race. The fishing boats are given a course to follow, and the skipper who most accurately forecasts the time it will take him to cover the course - without any adjustments to the engine speed - is judged the winner.

Our skipper, SJ, does a lot of engineering work for the fishing fleet, and he had been persuaded to take the Lady Jane along to watch the fun. We plunged about in the wake of the trawlers, enjoying ourselves, until it was time to put into port. The other pleasure craft tied up to moorings in the open harbour, but SJ brought Lady Jane alongside the fleet and we tied up to a friend of his in the Islander.

Her skipper Frank was a bouncy little man. He came aboard the Lady Jane and the serious side of the day began. SJ opened up a bottle of rum and tossed the cap overboard. "We won't be needing that again," he said, pouring Frank a generous measure.

Gradually, the Lady Jane began to rival the local pub, as more and more skippers and crew gathered on board. Our crewman Knot was despatched to get fresh supplies, and never returned - someone deposited him on his own front lawn sometime during the following night.

Eagle Eye and I were sent next. When we got back, there was a huge argument going on. They had got past the technical stage and the exchange seemed to consist of SJ saying: "Yes it can!" And someone else saying: "No it can't!"

SJ shouted at me: "Tell this ****!"

SJ's protagonist said: "You can't run this navigation system as a Decca without a special chip. That's all I;m saying. Tell this silly old \*\*\*\*\*\* that, and we can get on with some serious drinking."

Silence fell and the assembled masses looked at me expectantly. "Um, well, I have to go to the head," I said.

Outside the wheelhouse the argument raged. I heard SJ yell: "I bet you a thousand pounds!". This was getting very heavy. SJ never joked about money and I, as the operator, was sure to get the blame should the equipment not perform according to SJ's expectations. I sneaked out of the head, up the steps and fished the manual out from under the chart table. In the forward cabin I feverishly flicked through the pages, then I sauntered into the wheelhouse.

"Now, what's the problem?" I asked.

Colin, an electronics expert who worked on Frank's boat, burst out: "SJ has just bet me, in front of all these witnesses, that your nav system can operate Decca as she is."

"And you say it can't?" I asked.

"That's right," Colin said. "This Mark one needs a special chip, an electronic thing inside it," he explained condescendingly, "to make it operate in the Decca system. Without it this model doesn't receive the signals." Here he slapped my navigator contemptuously on its casing.

All this confidence was having an effect on SJ. His speech didn't give anything away, but it was obvious to the crowd that it was all bluster. He was in a corner and didn't know how to get out of it.

"Well go on then, show him," SJ commanded with some anxiety.

Change to red, then function eight, I reminded myself as I pressed the buttons. After an almost imperceptible pause a new set of information flashed on to the screen. It was all Greek to me but to these men who used Decca daily, the figures were instantly recognisable.

"Right," said Frank, "Pay the man, Colin." Colin sullenly muttered something about not having his cheque book with him and SJ asked chirpily if he wanted any help to find his way home for it.

After the laughter had died down, Colin said slyly: "I bet you can't use the Decca system, anyway."

SJ, flushed by success, rose to the challenge immediately. "We can find our way anywhere, using any system," he said.

The argument was joined again: "Up the red. Down the green." Phrases were being bandied about that made no sense whatsoever. A new bet was devised by Colin. Using only the Decca system we were to find our way home in the dark that night. I had a carefully programmed selection of waypoints in the memory - but Colin wiped these in about two minutes.

All the charts were taken on board Frank's boat and a new one was brought onto the Lady Jane. This was laid out for the Decca system, with different coloured lines sweeping across it.

A quick glance was all it took to convince SJ that there

was no problem. "All right," he said, shaking Colin's hand. "double or quits."

It should have been quite easy; even without any navigation aids we should have been able to find our way home blindfold. SJ sat with the chart and called out: "Follow red forty five until you hit the green," - stuff that he had heard on the radio when fishermen were lying to each other about their catches.

Sammy, on the wheel, said: "Aye, aye, skipper," and ignored him.

We had just entered the lough - forty minutes from Killybay - when the fog came down. It had been a little bit misty in the open sea, but this was a pea-souper. Eagle Eye went onto the bows with the foghorn and we gingerly felt our way towards home. "Switch the radar

"...Just shut up about your Decca, and lets get on with some serious drinking!"

on," SJ ordered Sammy.

"What about the bet?" Sammy asked, not realising the seriousness of the situation.

"Are you going to tell him?" SJ enquired.

With the radar, we could see that we were keeping a fairly straight course up the middle of the channel. Using my waypoints we could have skipped from one of these to the next - using the radar only to warn us of any other boats. As it was, we were forced to try to stay in the centre of the channel away from the dangers which, we knew, were further in.

Suddenly the fog lifted; only for a few minutes, but it gave Sammy a chance to see the light his eyes had been straining for. A slight adjustment brought us on course and we all felt assured of getting home.

The only problem was that there should have been another light dead astern, but no matter how hard we peered, we could not penetrate the murk. Eagle Eye, still on the bows, suddenly leapt to his feet and started yelling.

"What's wrong with him?" Sammy asked, but he did not reach for the throttles. I pushed past him and stuck my head out of the door. Eagle Eye was waving his arms about, jumping up and down and making gurgling noises.

I pulled both throttles full astern just as we struck. SJ, Mo and Old Bob had started to their feet, and they came tumbling up the wheelhouse as the Lady Jane grated to a halt, then back they slid as the deck rose in front of them.

We had hit the remains of an old dredger, sunk just at the edge of the channel. The smooth steel plates allowed the Lady Jane's steel hull to skid onto it. As the screws bit, we were dragged back into deep water, and Eagle Eye beat the dredger with a boat hook and shouted: "Get back, you ******!"

Moored safely in Killybay we checked for damage, found none, and prepared to go ashore. Normally the dinghy was tied to the bottom of the steps - unless it was tied to the side. SJ marched straight down the steps and into the sea. Sammy jumped in and managed to keep SJ afloat until Eagle Eye helped pull him into the dinghy. Slowly we motored in towards the quay, leaving Lady Jane waiting patiently for the next time we would come down to the sea.

**Also published by Fernhurst Books**